What's Cooking
in the
New Forest

Travelling
Gourmet
Publications

Travelling Gourmet Publications:

Cooking on the Move
A cookery book for caravanners, campavanners and boaters cooking in a
confined mobile kitchen. Price: 4.50

What's Cooking in the New Forest. Price 4.75

What's Cooking on the Isle of Wight. Second edition. Price 4.75

Published by: Travelling Gourmet Publications
Padmore Lodge, Beatrice Avenue
East Cowes, Isle of Wight

Edited by: Angela Hewitt
Illustrated by: The editor
Copy Right: What's Cooking Series: Travelling Gourmet Publications
Printed and bound in England by: Itchen Printers Ltd., Southampton

Price £4.75

This book is dedicated
to all those who believe small is beautiful, and to all
those individual food and catering businesses who
dedicate their lives to personally providing only the
best in food and service.

And to all of you; tourists and locals alike, who
support these businesses and by doing so keep our
unique heritage alive.

What's Cooking
in the
New Forest

Recipes from the best of The Forest's
Restaurants, Cafes, Tearooms, Pubs,
Producers and Suppliers.

The definitive guide to cooking,
shopping and eating out.

Contents

Introduction 7

The New Forest 9

Survival of the Forest 10

Starters 11

Light Lunches and Vegetarian Dishes 23

Fish and Shellfish 37

Meat, Poultry and Game 45

Puddings and Desserts 67

Afternoon Teas 77

Food Files:
The Shopping Basket	13
Watercress Beds	15
The Mushroom Hunt	18
Vegetarian Cookery	25
The Herb Garden	28
Wild Avon Salmon	39
Angling for a Fish	43
The Value of Meat	47
Pigs at Panage	51
Commoner's Rights	57
Royal Venison	63
Forest Vines	65
Autumn Forest Fruits	68
Self Pick Farms	70
Let's Bake a Cake	79
Xmas in the New Forest	83

Town and Village Guide	89
Index of Contributors	91
Measurements and Conversions	93
Index of Recipes	94

Cooking Notes

Oven Temperatures Vary particularly in fan ovens which can be hotter and should be reduced a notch. Old ovens can also vary. The temperatures in this book are only a guide to what the optimum oven should be.

Measurements should not be mixed. Stick to one or the other, imperial or metric.

Baking Blind means to line an uncooked pastry case with greaseproof paper or tin foil then fill with dried beans. This acts as a weight and prevents the pastry from rising in the centre and collapsing around the side during baking. The case should be cooked in a hot oven for 15-20 minutes or until the pastry is cooked and a pale golden colour.

Pastry is sometimes called for in a recipe without giving precise instructions. if 8oz-225gm of pastry is required, this means pastry made with 8oz-225gm of plain flour. If using ready made pastry then 12oz-350gm is usually required.

Bain Marie or Water Bath, is a large roasting pan or saucepan filled with hot water in which a smaller dish or basin containing the food is placed. The idea is to keep a difficult sauce i.e bernaise, warm, or to protect the sides of something delicate while it is being cooked in the oven, for instance a baked egg custard.

Introduction

It is already known that the New Forest has an international reputation for its excellent cuisine, and gourmets travel from far and wide to sample its tasty splendour. You will never go hungry or become disheartened by the sight of too much fast-food for everywhere you turn there is something good to eat. However, we discovered something else. While compiling this book we found not only a bounty of food but enormous generosity and abundant friendliness. (The invitations to drop in for coffee have been numerous. We hope they understand if we don't make it to all of them). Don't let anyone tell you the South of England is stand-offish.

We couldn't have hoped for a finer collection of recipes. The wide variety in this book clearly demonstrates the wealth of cooking talent that exists in the New Forest area. Most of the recipes are of the chefs' own creation and the only real problem was writing them down, having cooked the dish for years by instinct alone.

Many of the restaurants are award winning, yet even those that aren't have something important to say, either about their wonderful food, about the care they take, the atmosphere they provide or the friendly, welcoming, service they have to give.

It is obvious that the New Forest people are proud of their little piece of England and want their visitors to experience the same pleasures.

They say that it is difficult for a cook to think in business terms, because instinctively they like to give - cooking comes from the heart. If this is true then there is an awful lot of heart in the New Forest.

Happy Eating!

Note to Eaters

The recipes in this book are an example of the kind of cuisine served at each
establishment.
Most chefs cook by instinct and use what is seasonally available;
therefore, the recipes found in this book are not always featured on their
menus.
However, there is always something equally as delicious to be found
in its place.

Restaurant Law. When you make a reservation, even by phone, you are entering a legal contract.
If for some reason you are unable to keep that reservation please let them know. No matter how short
the notice. At least you are giving them a chance to resell the table to a casual caller. Failure to do so
could incur a cancellation fee. So, don't spoil your holiday, please let them know.

The New Forest

There is something rather pleasant, like little bubbles of excitement, about driving through a village or along a country lane and coming across a family of wild ponies ambling contentedly through their day. The feeling is sort of catching, and I think you'll agree it is far more thrilling to see ponies and other farm animals like this, free to mingle with the crowds rather than confined behind unfriendly barriers. It is this sight alone that brings thousands of tourists to the New Forest.

Despite its name the New Forest is far from new, and as far as 'The Forest' goes, a great deal of it is heathland. Nevertheless, it is a bewitching place, full of enough romanticism for everyone, from the tiniest child to the last of the octaganerians. Its beauty comes from within and to experience it you need to leave your car, put on your best walking shoes and explore the many tracks that lead into The Forest.

You are asked to forgive the keepers of The Forest for putting what at first seems tight restrictions upon the tourists pleasure, but it is thanks to them that so many of us can freely enjoy the delights of this delightfully preserved area. There a numerous sympathetically designed car-parks thoughtfully positioned so that there is easy access into the forest and an extraordinary network of footpaths have been created, some well off the beaten-track, for everyones pleasure.

It is a nature lover's paradise and the changing shades of the forest provide seasonal delights throughout the year: from deep verdant green in the heart of summer to the rich purples and oranges of autumn - for some the most beautiful time. Bright golds and rich browns are cast throughout the winter leading us into the bright, fresh greens and yellows as the season turns to spring.

The Forest's basin runs down to the southern coast where sea-side fun can be yet another family pleasure. Water features strongly in the New Forest; from the casual, sensual, flow of rivers and streams to the tranquillity of ponds and pools. You might like to fish with a rod or net, or simply picnic on a leafy river bank, or try a little sailing or rowing across one of the inland lakes or ponds.

On a rainy day there is no shortage of places to find a nice pot of tea or a good pint. There are plenty of historical and natural history to discover and a hive full of arts and craft to explore, depending on your interests, while you shelter for a few hours until the sun emerges to cast its summery light through the leafy bowers.

The Survival of the Forest

The New Forest is a designated conservation area. It is one of the last reserves where ancient history, that of the "Commoner's rights", is still vigourously in progress, a real living-history!.

Sadly, over the years the influx of tourists, eager to experience the joys of the forest have also been the source of a loss of grazing. Car oil dropped on grass, fires lit, grass worn bare by cricket and football games and wheel skids all cause an erosion which can take up to a month to regenerate. Multiply this by thousands and you can soon see how quickly grazing land can disappear.

This problem has been controlled by organising designated camping sites, parking facilities and general access into The Forest via walkways and scenic drives. You may be disappointed by these restrictions but be reassured that this is why people can still be welcomed into The Forest. Remember, the New Forest is as much a part of our National Heritage as any stately home.

Visitors can help.

A few simple self imposed rules can ensure that The Forest will be a pleasure for everyone for many years to come.

Many of the roads are unfenced and ponies and farm stock, who have no road sense at all are prone to wonder aimlessly across. A speed limit of 40mph, particularly at night, will not only reduce the death toll of ponies, deer and cattle but will curtail accidents and damage to your car. When parking, use one of the 150 free Forest car parks and avoid the verges which cause damage to the natural environment.

Don't forget the ponies and donkeys are wild animals and can be at times dangerous. There is plenty of natural food for them within The Forest and although it might seem a delight to hand feed a pony you are doing them no favours and they could be lured onto dangerous roads unnecessarily while looking for easy food. Also they can bite, literally, the hand that feeds them.

Dogs and The Forest just don't mix. Keep them under control and on a lead at all times.

You are welcome, indeed encouraged to walk on any of the footpaths or tracks winding through The Forest; but please keep to the paths so that wild life is not disturbed.

Fire is a serious threat to The Forest, therefore camp fires are not allowed. If you wish to have a picnic or barbeque do so at one of the numerous, (over 80) designated picnic and barbeque sites.

Finally, ponies are not as intelligent as humans and they have been killed by the reckless eating of plastic bags etc. Don't put yourself in a position where you might have been the cause of such a tragedy, always take your rubbish home with you in a refuse bag. *Happy holidaying.*

Starters

As a prelude to a larger meal a starter should be small, light and appetising. Something to whet the appetite and stimulate the gastric juices.

Many of the starters in this section can be served as a light snack or lunch by increasing the proportions and accompanying with a crisp, lightly dressed salad and freshly baked bread.

When choosing your starter, most important of all is a question of balance. For instance, avoid serving two cream based dishes together, and if you are serving two fish dishes try and make one of them shell fish.

For ease, soup is by far the best option. It can be prepared in advance then re-heated at the last minute. If soup is to be hot make sure it is piping and if cold it should be icy cold.

Whatever your choice, remember a starter is not to be made a meal of, and the emphasis should be on "little and light".

Spiced Parsnip and Peanut Soup

An unusual and 'morish' soup

2 onions chopped
4 celery stalks, sliced
3lb-1.4kg parsnips, peeled and diced
2oz-50gm butter
1/2 tspn chilli powder
5pts-2.8lt vegetable stock
6oz-175gm crunchy peanut butter
1 tspn lemon juice
1 tspn dark soya sauce

1...Gently fry the onions, celery and parsnips for about 5 minutes.
2...Stir in chilli powder and cook for 1 minute.
3...Add the stock, peanut butter, lemon juice, soya sauce and seasoning and bring to the boil. Reduce heat. Cover, then simmer for 30 minutes until the vegetables are nice and soft.
4...Cool slightly, then puree in a food processor. Do this in two batches. Re-heat gently and serve with brown crusty bread or naan bread.

From the kitchen of...

THE BROCK AND BRUIN TEAROOM
25 Brookley Road Brockenhurst. Tel: 01590 622020
Proprietors: Jane and Graham Overall
Chefs: Jane Overall and Sarah Buck
Open: All year 10am - 6pm. Closed Christmas.
Serving: Morning coffee, light lunches and afternoon tea.
Casual callers and children welcome. Licensed. Non-Smoking.
Enjoy their wonderful home-made food including a wide range of splendid cakes while sitting amongst the badgers and bears.

The Shopping Basket

It is a sad fact that if we don't support our local shops and small producers they will disappear without trace.

The convenience of the supermarket has beguiled us all and yet their fresh produce such as meat, vegetables and bread, food we would normally have bought from the butcher, the baker and the green grocer, is more expensive to buy at the supermarket.

It's true that the supermarket has the edge where groceries are concerned, but that is where it begins and ends. An important area where the supermarket falls down is in its disinterest in promoting local produce; for example speciality ice creams, chocolates, biscuits, chutneys etc.

When you are on holiday with more time on your hands, and a slower pace to your schedule, you can find the time to search out these small shops and enjoy the traditional pleasures of being served all that delicious local food. There's no shadow of a doubt it has been prepared with loving care, not for the masses but for you, the individual.

It should be noted that it isn't the supermarkets that are innovative, but the small producer and creative chef that are behind all that is new on the shelves at these mass markets.

The New Forest is renowned for its game, particularly venison, although there is plenty of pheasant, mallard and partridge. Other game such as grouse, snipe and widgeon can also be found. For the very best meat there is Hockey's at Fordingbridge. They farm to traditional methods and sell their organically reared meat and other produce from their farm shop. As well as locally caught fish from the sea, wild salmon from the river Avon is delicious. Local ice-cream, hand-made chocolates, fresh herbs and watercress and an excellent locally produced and bottled table wine are readily available in many shops throughout The Forest.

To keep this bounty of produce alive it is essential that we support our small local shops and producers. The small shopkeeper is part of our National Heritage. Apart from that we desperately need them and the competition they give the big boys. If they are forced to close through lack of business it is inevitable that supermarkets will have a monopoly and general food prices will climb sky high.

Great Britain has some of the best food in the world and the most humanely produced. Don't let anyone tell you otherwise. "What's Cooking" is here to tell you why it is the best, and to promote those that serve the best!

Watercress Soup

One of England's most traditional and elegant soups

1/2lb-225gm old potatoes
2pts-1.1lt good chicken stock
2 large bunches of very fresh watercress
salt and black pepper
2 or 3 tbls whipping cream, according to taste

1...Peel the potatoes and cut in half. Cook the potatoes in the chicken stock, (use a stainless steel or enamel lined saucepan), until the potatoes fall. Remove from the heat.
2...Add the two bunches of watercress, (elastic bands removed). Stand for about ten minutes off the heat. The tender cress will cook in the residual heat. It is essential that the cress is not boiled as it tends to turn black.
3...Put in a blender and whizz until smooth.
4...Return to a gentle heat and add the whipping cream. The more cream you add the more delicate the flavour. Serve with crispy croutons.

From the kitchen of...

THE QUEENS HEAD
The Cross, Burley, Nr Ringwood. Tel: 01425 403423
Proprietor: Wayside Inns
Manager: Paul Nippard
Open: All year. All day. 11am - 11pm. Food from 12noon.
Casual callers and children welcome. Credit cards. Outside seating. Log Fire in winter.
Home-style baking. Pies, game dishes, delicious soups. Vegetarian dishes. Seasonal seafood. Regular changing blackboard menu.
The three resident donkeys, Doris, Dilly and Daisy are attuned to the sound of crisps. Dogs allowed. A central point for Forest walks.

Watercress Beds

What is watercress? A herb or a salad leaf? It could be either, yet sadly it is more often than not relegated to the garnish on the plate.

It has a hot, tangy, refreshing taste and makes a wonderful soup or sauce to go with fish, chicken and even lamb. Watercress sandwiches were once a popular tea time dish. In today's modern cookery there have been watercress mousses, watercress roulades and watercress stuffing. It has a high proportion of vitamin C and much of its strong flavour comes from it high iron content. It is without doubt good for you.

Watercress grows in fresh, running water, where the soil has a high lime content. Alresford on the river Avon and on the outskirts of the New Forest is considered watercress country. Large flat beds fed with spring water are laid to thick, green carpets of watercress. At a glance you could think you were among the paddy fields of Asia.

The watercress is mainly harvested during late autumn, winter and early spring. This is when it is at its best.

Once harvested, if not stored properly it has a short shelf life and leaves turn quickly yellow. To store, put the bunches of watercress in a plastic bag, squeeze out as much air as you possibly can and put in the fridge. I have kept watercress successfully for up to four days this way. Because of the iron content in watercress cook it in stainless steel or enamelled saucepans; and when cooking don't boil the leaves as excessive heat tends to turn them black.

Warm Watercress Tartlets with Stilton Sauce

A elegant starter which can also be served as a vegetarian luncheon dish.

1 bunch bright green watercress
1 medium potato, peeled and cooked
1 small onion
2 large eggs
1/2pt double cream
salt and pepper
pinch freshly grated nutmeg
8oz-225gm short pastry made with: 8oz-225gm plain flour, 3oz-75gm
butter, 2oz-50gm lard, 1 small egg.
<u>*Stilton sauce*</u>
4oz-110gm stilton cheese
1/4pt-150gm white wine
1/4pt-150ml stock
8fl oz-200ml double cream
pepper, pinch freshly grated nutmeg

1...Make the pastry. Chill in the fridge for at least 20 minutes before using. Divide the pastry into four pieces and roll out each portion into a circle large enough to line a small 3" quiche tin. Bake blind in a pre-heated oven 200c/400f.gas6 for 15 minutes or until pale and golden.
2...Wash the watercress and remove any 'woody' stems. Roughly chop and put in an enamel or stainless steel saucepan with the onion and the potato. Add a drop of oil. Cover tightly and steam over a very low heat until the watercress has wilted.
3...Tip into a blender and add the two eggs, the 1/2pt of double cream and seasoning. Blend until smooth.
4...Spoon the mixture into the pre-cooked pastry cases and return to the oven. 190c/375f/gas5 for about 30 minutes or until the watercress mixture is set.
5...Keep warm while you make the sauce: Put the white wine and stock in a saucepan and reduce by half. Lower the temperature. Grate the stilton cheese and add to the white wine. Cook gently until the cheese has melted. Add the cream and bring to the boil. Add seasoning.
6...Remove the tartlets from their rings and place on warm plates. Garnish with a small bouquet of leaves and a few green grapes and pour around the sauce.

Mushroom Barquette

A starter for two. Double up the proportions for four

4oz-110gm small button mushrooms
1oz-25gm butter
2 tbls brandy
2oz-50 grm shallots
1 clove garlic
1 tbls chopped fresh chives
2 tbls double cream
2 individual savoury short crust pastry cases
watercress to garnish

1...Place the pastry cases on their serving plates and pop in a warm oven.
2...Finely chop the shallot and garlic then saute in the melted butter until soft but not brown.
3...Wipe over the button mushrooms (keep them whole) add to the shallots and saute for about 5 minutes.
4...Add the brandy and flame.
5...Pour in the double cream, bring to the boil then add the chopped chives.
6...Remove warm pastry cases from the oven, spoon in the mushroom mixture and garnish. Serve immediately.

From the menu of...

CARRIAGES RESTAURANT
At String of Horses
Mead End Road. Sway. Nr Lymington. Tel: 01590 682631
Proprietor: Mrs G A Reardon.
Chef: Mr Julio Frias-Robles
Open: All year. Wed - Sat 7pm - 9pm and Sunday Luncheon 12.30 - 2pm
Booking Essential. Credit cards accepted. Seafood and vegetarian dishes.
Non-smoking restaurant.
In the evenings enjoy a romantic candlelit dinner in sumptuous surroundings.

The Mushroom Hunt

The New Forest is well known nationally as a rich source for wild mushrooms and people travel from as far as London to search out these earth borne specimens. Indeed, in recent years there has been some concern about the amount of commercial foragers who are gathering mushrooms by the hamper load and shipping them back to London restaurants. Recent local publicity has been mounted to reduce this indiscriminate gathering. The aim being to return the mushroom collecting pursuit to the judicious pleasures of the local population who gather just a few for their own personal consumption.

A wild mushroom identification book is an essential tool, as is a cautious nature. They say there are only two truly deadly mushrooms in this country, but that should be enough to make you check and double check before eating them. On top of that there numerous species that will make you ill and even some edible ones will make a sensitive stomach revolt. The shaggy ink cap is quite delicious and makes a tasty dinner party sauce. But! if eaten with alcohol you will suffer sever palpitations and unpleasant hallucinations.

It is easy to feel romantic about foraging for mushrooms, but if there is any doubt in your mind then leave well alone. Instead, buy your wild fungi at a local delicatessen where they have been picked and packed by experts.

Dried mushrooms do seem expensive, yet they have such a powerful flavour only a few are required to elevate a simple mushroom dish to something quite outstanding. The most common varieties are morels and ceps and half an ounce is sufficient to enhance the flavour of a pound of cultivated mushrooms.

Soak dried mushrooms in a basin of hot water and stand for 3-4 hours. Morels tend to carry bits of grit amongst their folds, so once they have reconstituted remove the mushrooms from the water and strain the liquid through a fine sieve. Retain the liquid and use as stock.

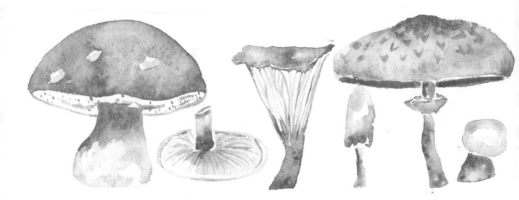

Wild Mushroom and Marjoram Soup

Delicious to serve at an autumn dinner party that might precede a game dish.

1lb-450gm open capped mushrooms
2 onions
2 cloves garlic, chopped
1/2oz dried ceps
1.3/4pts-1litre chicken or vegetable stock
freshly milled black pepper, lots
salt
2 tbls freshly chopped marjoram
2-3 tbls cream
oil

1...Put the dried mushrooms in a basin and pour over enough boiling water to cover. Stand for three or four hours.
2...Finely chop the onions and soften in a little oil. Slice the mushrooms and add to the onions. Add the chopped garlic. Cook gently until the mushrooms have collapsed.
3...Scoop the ceps out of their liquid and add to the mushrooms in the pan. Strain the ceps' liquid to remove any grit and add liquid to the pan. Add the stock and marjoram. Cover and simmer for about 30 minutes.
4...Put the soup through the blender. Return to a clean saucepan. Add plenty of freshly milled black pepper, a pinch of salt according to taste and the cream.
Serves 4.

Wessex Mussels

Serve with hot crusty roll and butter. Serves 5-6 people.

6pts-3kilos whole shell on mussels
1/2pt-275ml water
1oz-25gm butter
2 cloves garlic, minced
1/4pt-150ml sherry
8oz-225gm mushrooms, finely chopped
4oz-110gm onions, finely chopped
4oz-110gm fresh white breadcrumbs
juice of one lemon
1oz-25gm chopped parsley plus extra for serving
salt and pepper
cayenne pepper
2 egg yolks, beaten
1/2pt-275ml double cream

1…Scrub and wash the mussels. Place in a large pan with the water. Cover and cook over a high heat until the shells open. Once the heat penetrates they begin to open very quickly.
2…Strain off the liquor and reserve. Remove one half of each mussel shell and the beards. Put to one side.
3…Heat the butter and lightly fry the onions, garlic and mushrooms.
4…Add the breadcrumbs, lemon juice, cooking juice, parsley, sherry salt and pepper to taste. Bring to the boil and simmer for 5 minutes.
5…Add the beaten egg yolks, cream and mussels. Heat thoroughly but do not boil. Pile into dishes and sprinkle with parsley and the cayenne pepper.

From the kitchen of…

NEW FOREST INN
Emery Down. Lyndhurst. Hants Tel: 01703 282329
Proprietors: Michael Grove and Wendy Cole
Chef: Ray
Open: All year 11am - 11pm. Christmas day normal Sunday hours.
Casual callers and well behaved children welcome. Credit cards accepted. Wheelchair access. Log fires in Winter and outside seating in Summer. Delicious food available all day including Sundays. Seafood and vegetarian dishes. Specialities, Fresh Crab Thermidore and Fillet of Pork in Cashew-nut and Cream sauce.

Ashlett Smokie

12oz-350gm smoked haddock
6oz-150gm small mushrooms thinly sliced
8oz-225gm strong cheddar cheese, grated
1/2pt-275ml white wine, medium or sweet
2 tbls double cream
1oz-25gm butter and 1oz-25gm flour to thicken sauce
knob of butter for cooking
salt and pepper

4 ramekin dishes

1...Remove the skin from the haddock and cut into cubes. Place in a non-metalic dish suitable for the microwave. Pour over the wine. Cover the dish and cook on high (650 power oven) until the fish is cooked through.
2...Melt the knob of butter and lightly saute the mushrooms. Put to one side.
3...Drain the fish and break into flakes. Retain the liquid.
4...Mix the fish with the mushrooms and put to one side while you make the sauce.
5...Melt the buter in a saucepan and add the flour. Cook through without browning for a few minutes then add the reserved fish liquid stirring all the time to make a stiff white sauce. Add 4oz-110gm of the grated cheese. Add the cream to enrich the sauce, but not too much cream as the sauce must remain thick.
6...Add the sauce to the haddock and mushrooms and mix. Divide the mixture between the ramekins. Cover the tops with the remaining grated cheese.
7...At this stage the ramekins can be kept in the fridge until ready to serve. To serve: Pop the ramekins in the microwave oven and re-heat. Then place under a hot grill until the tops are a delicious golden brown.

From the menu of...

THE JOLLY SAILOR
Victoria Quay. Ashlett Creek. Fawley. Hants. Tel: 01703 891305
Proprietors: Tony and Sue Redfern.
Open: Winter - All day opening Friday and Saturday. Summer All day opening every weekday.
Children and dogs are welcome and wheelchairs are easily accommodated.
A wide-spread reputation has grown for their good food in both the two bars and restaurant. Delicious Roast Carvery is served on Sunday from October to May. Friendly, welcoming surroundings decorated with many nautical themes. Gentle live music played Friday and Sunday. Real Ales on tap. The picnic tables outside overlooks the yacht club and the many boats of visiting yachtsmen.

Scallops in Basil Butter Sauce

From Ian McAndrew's book A Feast of Fish. This recipe is a particular favourite of his - the fresh basil really complements the delicate flavour of the scallops.

20-24 scallops
salt and freshly ground white pepper
1/2pt-300ml fish stock
1fl oz-20ml dry sherry
12 fresh basil leaves, shredded
5oz-150gm cold unsalted butter

1...Shell, trim and wash the scallops. Dry well. Season and poach gently in the fish stock and sherry for 2-3 minutes. Do not allow the liquid to boil or the scallops will over cook and become dry very quickly. When cooked, remove from cooking stock, cover and keep warm.

2...To make the sauce. Reduce the liquor to a quarter of its original volume and add the basil leaves. Bring the sauce to the boil then immediately reduce the heat to very low. Now gradually add the butter, whisking continuously until it has melted. Be careful not to let the sauce boil once the butter has gone in or it will separate. The butter will thicken the sauce and give it a smooth velvety texture. Season to taste.

To serve:- Arrange the scallops in warm (not hot) soup plates and pour over the sauce. Garnish if wished with short crust pastry shells.

Serves 6-8.

From the kitchen of...

THE BOAT HOUSE
Bar/Brasserie
Shamrock Way. Hythe Marina Village. Hythe. Tel: 01703 845594
Proprietors: Ian and Jane McAndrew
Chef: Ian McAndrew. Mitchelin Star. Cookery Writer.
Open: All year. Winter 11am - 3pm and 6am - 11pm. Longer hours during the summer months.
Booking advised in the brasserie but casual callers welcome if there's room. Children welcome. Most credit cards. Wheelchair access. Outside seating and River views. Seafood and Vegetarian Dishes.
Outstanding food. Must not be missed.

Light Lunches
and
Vegetarian Dishes

Most of the recipes in this section can be served either as a starter or a main course simply by increasing or decreasing the proportions. Because it is lunch and not a main meal of the day it is recommended that these recipes are served with a lightly dressed side salad.

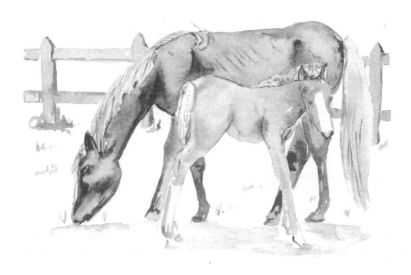

New Forest Pasty

A home-made pasty suitable for vegetarians and a superb pub snack for all.

8oz-225gm button mushrooms, sliced
6oz-175gm wild mushrooms or oyster mushrooms
4oz-110gm mixed nuts (optional)
1 onion
2 sticks celery
1/2 small bulb fennel
2 cloves garlic
1 tspn mixed herbs
8fl oz white wine
8fl oz double cream
oil or butter for cooking
shortcrust pastry made from: 8oz-225gm plain flour, 4oz-110gm butter,
1 egg, pinch of salt, water to bind.

1…Make the pastry and place in the fridge to rest.
2…Finely dice the onion, celery, fennel and garlic then cook until soft in a little butter or oil.
3…Add the sliced mushrooms and wild mushrooms, mixed nuts and herbs and continue to cook.
4…When cooked add the white wine and reduce by half.
5…Add the double cream and reduce again by half. Season to taste with salt and ground black pepper. Leave to cool.
6…Roll out the pastry to approx 6"-15cm rounds (depending on required size). Place a spoonful of the cooled mushroom mixture in the centre and form the pasty.
7…Brush with egg wash, place on a flat baking sheet and bake 200c/400f/gas6 until golden brown. Serve with a mixed salad.

From the menu of…

THE BELL INN
At Bramshaw Golf Club
Brook. Bramshaw. Tel: 01703 812214/ Fax: 01703 813958
Manager: Mr Gavin Scott
Chef: Mr Malcolm Lugg
Open: All year including Christmas. Winter 12 - 2.30. and 6.30 - 9.30. Summer 12 noon - 9.30.
Casual callers and children welcome. Wheelchair access. Outside seating and log fire in winter.
Specialising in fresh local game and seafood. Vegetarian dishes. Home-made style soups, Terrines, pasta dishes and sweets.

Vegetarian Cookery

Vegtarianism has become an emotive subjectg, and a great deal of intolerance goes with it on both side of the argument. Of course there is no argument you either choose to be a vegetarian or not, and some vegetarians go further than others. This refusal to understand the vegetarian tends to blend with the few vegetarians who try to ram their beliefs down the throats of others. Their self-righteous attitude niggles, and 'those others' throw back strongly weighted questions that enter the grey areas of vegetarianism. It all causes considerable antagonism; when really we should be grateful we have the choice.

Nevertheless, there are more vegetarians in England today than ever, especially amongst the younger generation. They constitute four percent of the population and their needs are willingly recognized in cafes, restaurants and pubs all over the country. Not only that, it's not just an omelette any more, dishes have become creative and substantial, although understandably the choice is small. Some dishes have been so imaginatively conceived that even non-vegetarians will eat a vegetarian meal at lunch time.

There are advantages to vegetarian cookery. It is quick and easy, (no more waiting for the roast to cook) and it is highly suitable to microwave cookery. Vegetarian food is fresh tasting and full of roughage. The one thing it does lack is essential ascorbic acid, normally derived from meat, but it can be obtained from mushrooms.

Vegetarianism has to be approached sensibly. Vegetables, unlike meat and dairy produce have no protein which is essential for the development of the body, and if a vegetarian is involved in manual work the body needs to be strong. Protein can be obtained from nuts, but one nut to be carefully measured is coconut which has high cholesterol forming fats.

Pulses, pasta and pastry are great vehicles for vegetarian meals and the vegetables provide a colourful and tempting repast. There's also a wide variety of cheeses available for the less strict vegetarian, and many new ways of serving them other than just grated onto a bed of lettuce. In fact there is no shortage of ingredients available to ensure a healthy, interesting, tasty vegetarian diet.

Tuscan Pie

1lb-450gm shortcrust pastry: Made with 1lb-450gm plain flour, 10oz-275gm fat, 1 beaten egg and a drop of cold water
1 large red capsicum
1 large green capsicum
2 courgettes
1 small aubergine
8 tomatoes
1lb-450gm pumpkin
1lb-450gm ricotta cheese
2oz-50gm
2 tbls fresh sage
salt and pepper

Cake tin 2"-5cm deep x 8"-20.5cm diameter

1...Make up the pastry and put to rest in the fridge.
2...Prepare the vegetables. Cut the peppers in half, remove the seeds, brush with oil, grill and then remove the skins. Cut the tomatoes in half and remove the seeds. Slice the courgettes into 1/4"-0.5cm thick. Slice the aubergines to the same thickness, put in a colander and sprinkle with salt and stand for 1 hour to remove the bitter juices, then saute in hot oil. Remove the tough skin from the pumpkin and cut into 1/4" slices then steam until tender.
3...Divide the pastry into two parts, one part a third larger than the other. Roll out the large part to fit the bottom and sides of the cake tin.
4...Assemble together the vegetables and the two cheeses and sage and make colourful layers with them in the cake tin, starting with a layer of pumpkin. On top of each layer put either a few knobs of ricotta cheese, a sprinkle of sage leaves or a sprinkling of parmesan cheese. Lightly season each layer.
5...Roll out the small pweice of pastry and place ontop of the pie. Seal down the edges. Brush with egg wash.
6...Place in a pre-heated oven 220c/425f/gas7 and bake for 20 minutes. Lower the heat to 180c/350f/gas 4 and bake for a further 20 minutes. Remove from oven and allow to cool.
Serve cold with an oil dressed side salad.

N.B. Other vegetables such as fennel, mushrooms, artichokes, carrots, etc can also be used. But keep it colourful.

Prawn Creole

Prawns in ratatouille with a cheese topping. Also delicious as a starter.

2 tbls oil
2 cloves garlic, crushed
2 large onions, sliced
1 aubergines, sliced
6 courgettes, sliced
1 green pepper, de-seeded
1.1/2lb-700gm tomatoes, skinned and sliced
salt and pepper
2 tbls tomato puree
1lb-450gm peeled prawns
8oz-225gm cheddar cheese, grated

1...Heat the oil in a pan then add the garlic and onions and cook for 5 minutes. Stirring occasionally.
2...Add the aubergines, courgettes, and pepper. Stir. Then add the tomatoes. Season with salt and pepper according to taste. Bring to the boil and simmer for 20 minutes.
3...Add the tomato puree and cook for 10 minutes
4...Add the peeled prawns (if using frozen defrost first). Turn into a casserole dish. Sprinkle over the grated cheese.
5...Put under a grill and grill until the cheese has melted and is golden. Serve with a side salad and crusty bread.

From the menu of...

BOSUNS CHAIR
Station Street. Lymington. Tel: 01590 675140
Proprietors: John and Carole Speary
Chef: Carole Speary
Open: All year except Christmas. Winter 11am - 3pm and 5.3-pm - 11pm. Summer 11am - 11pm
Casual callers and children welcome. Credit cards accepted. Wheelchair access. Outside seating.
Lively Pub and Bistro with live music every Sunday evening.
Vegetarian dishes, and always the ever popular, garlic bread, Pint of Prawns, Steak au Poivre and Egg Florentine.

The Herb Garden

The use of herbs in cookery goes as far back as the history of food has ever been recorded. For a long time tradition told us what herbs went best with which food. For example sage and onion stuffing with pork, mint sauce with lamb, tarragon with chicken, parsley with fish. However, as is always the case, things change, rules get broken and now, in the late twentieth century the domestic kitchen has become a huge laboratory of experimentation. Herb cookery is all over the place as we try swopping around the flavours, some old, others quite new to us. Modern English cookery is mixing, for example, French cookery with Indian cookery, and Thai cookery with English cookery; It is all very exciting.

Gardeners too are paying more attention to the flavourings, finding larger corners to grow their garden of herbs amongst the rows of vegetables. The old tradition of a knot garden made from fragrant herbs is beginning to form a small oasis in the modern ornamental garden.

Lymore Valley herb garden, just two miles from Hurst Castle, demonstrates how easily a delightful herb garden can be created. Visitors are welcome to explore the gardens and gather ideas on their way. They have a well stocked plant centre where you can purchase many unusual herbs and a herb shop in one of the barns where there are many herb inspired products. Above the shop is the Tennyson room where throughout the year may find anything from an exhibition of South American Tribal art to a cookery demonstration by a well known personality.

Lymore Valley Herbs Pesto Sauce.

2 cups fresh basil
1/2 cup fresh parsley
1/2 cup olive oil
1 tbls pine nuts
1 tspn salt
1/2 cup grated Parmesan cheese

Puree together in a blender the first five ingredients. Then stir in the cheese. It's as simple as that! Best used fresh with pasta or as a salsa to go with fish or meat.

It will keep in the fridge for three days.

Pizza Tart 1990

Individual tarts can also be made from this recipe

6 sheets filo pastry
olive oil
1 red pepper
1 green pepper
1 yellow pepper
2 beefsteak tomatoes
1 red onion, sliced
3 cloves garlic, cut into thin slivers
1 tbls capers
small bunch fresh basil leaves
4oz-110gm mozarellas cheese
2oz-50gm fresh Parmesan cheese, in one piece
1 tbls tomato puree

1   Cut the peppers into quarters. Brush the skins with olive oil and grill skin side up until they start to go black. Cover with a tea-towel while removing the charred skins. Put to one side.
2   Brush the filo sheets with olive oil and use the sheets to line a 10inch-25cm shallow flan ring.
3   Spread the tomato paste over the base of the flan ring. Tear up some basil leaves and scatter over the tomato puree. Cut the mozarellas into thin slivers and scatter on top. Slice the tomatoes and arrange on top of the cheese. Scatter over more torn basil and the slivers of garlic. Now scatter over the prepared quarters of peppers and red onion slices.
4   Finnish off with any left over mozarellas cheese and a scattering of capers. Place in a hot oven gas7/425f/220c and bake for 20-30 minutes.
5   Remove from the oven. Shave the Parmesan into wafer thin curls with a potato peeler and scatter over the pizza tart. Serve with a simple dressed salad. Serves 4.

Dairy Quiche

*shortcrust pastry made from: - 6oz-175gm plain flour, 2oz-50gm
wholemeal flour, 4oz-110gm butter, 1/4 tspn salt and cold water
4oz-110gm streaky bacon
small onion, finely chopped
1/4pt fresh dairy milk
1/4pt fresh dairy single cream
4 size 2 eggs, well beaten
2oz-50gm mature cheddar cheese, grated
salt and pepper*

1...Make up the shortcrust pastry. Roll out in a round large enough to line a
9" lightly greased flan dish. Prick the base and bake-blind in a pre-heated
oven 190c/375f/gas 5 for 10-15 minutes until dry.
2...Cut the bacon into small strips and place in a pan with the chopped onion
and fry gently in its own fat until soft. Drain thoroughly on kitchen paper.
3...Put the bacon and onion in the bottom of the prepared case and top with
half the cheddar cheese.
4...Heat the milk and cream to just below boiling point and whisk into the
eggs. Season with salt and pepper.
5...Pour into the pastry case and sprinkle with the remainder of the cheese.
6...Bake in the centre of the oven for 15 minutes and then reduce the heat to
160c/325f/gas3 for a further 30-40 minutes or until the filling is set. Serve
hot.
Serves five to six people.

Recipe supplied by...

PENSWORTH FARMS
Milkhills Farm. Goggs Lane. Redlynch. Salisbury. Wiltshire. SP5 2NY
Tel: 01725 510437
Office Manager: Mrs C Somerset
Suppliers of fresh dairy milk, cream, butter, cheese, eggs and yogurt to hotels, cafes, restaurants and
retail shops. Phone for details.

Baked Egg and Smoked Ham en Cocotte

A simple and delicious dish using the best dairy produce.

4 size 1 eggs
8oz-225gm smoked, cooked ham, diced
2 tbls finely chopped onion, softened in butter
8 tbls double cream, (approx) must be double
4oz-110gm mature cheddar cheese, (be generous)
salt and pepper

1...Pre-heat oven to its highest setting
2...Divide the onion between four large cocotte dishes. Arrange the diced ham around the edge of the dish, leaving a hollow in the centre.
3...Break 1 egg in the centre of each hollow, then pour over the cream, about 2 tbls per cocotte.
4...Grate the cheddar and sprinkle generous amounts on top.
5...Place the cocottes on a baking tray and put in the oven for 15-20 minutes depending how well you like your eggs done.
To serve: put a folded napkin on a plate and serve immediately. Garnish with a sprig of fresh herbs.

Variations - smoked haddock, cooked leeks, sauted mushrooms, cooked spinach, chopped tomatoes, prawns, left over bolognaise./ Stilton cheese, goats milk cheese, roqueforte cheese, emmental and gruyer cheese.

Croft Lasagne

A traditional tasty pub recipe made special by the addition of red wine.

12oz-350gm lean minced beef
1 large onion chopped
2 tbls oil
1 hpd tspn dried oregano
1 or 2 cloves garlic crushed with a little salt
1/2pt red wine
4 sticks celery, chopped
1 tin Italian chopped tomatoes
1/2 small tin tomato puree
salt and pepper
Cheese Sauce - 1oz-25gm flour, 1oz-25gm butter plus 1 tbls oil, good
1/2pt-275ml milk, 6oz-175gm mature cheddar
12 sheets dried lasagne pasta.
4 fresh tomatoes

1...Heat the oil in a frying pan and cook the celery, onion and garlic until
golden. Add the mince and cook until turning brown. Add the oregano,
tinned tomatoes, tomato puree, red wine and seasoning and simmer gently for
thirty minutes until the sauce reduces and becomes thicker.
2...Meanwhile make the cheese sauce. Melt the butter and oil in a saucepan
and add the flour. Cook for one minute without browning. Add the milk and
stir all the time until the sauce thickens. Grate the cheese and add 4oz-110gm
to the sauce. Cook gently until the cheese has melted.
3...Spread some of the meat mixture over the bottom of an oblong casserole
dish. Top with three pasta sheets. Continue until the beef and pasta is used up.
End with a pasta sheet.
4...Pour the cheese sauce over the pasta. Arrange sliced tomato on top and
sprinkle over remaining cheese. (If the pasta is not the easy to use type, let the
dish stand for thirty minutes so that the sauce begins to soften the pasta.) Bake
in a pre-heated oven. 200c/400f/gas 6 for 20-30 minutes until the top is golden
brown and bubbling. Serve with crusty bread, green salad.
From the menu of...

THE CROFT TAVERN
Langtown Lawn. Hythe. Hants. Tel:01703 842141
Manager: Lynn Stuart-Murray
Open: All year 11am - 11pm. Sunday 12 - 3pm and 7pm - 10.30pm.
Credit cards accepted. Children welcome in the large garden with play area. Separate restaurant. Log fire.
Good traditional home cooking. Vegetarian dishes. Real Ales.

Leeks and Ham au Gratin

Serve as individual portions with side salad. Best made in the winter when leeks are at their best.

2 small leeks per person or 1 large leek cut in half
2 thick slices of ham per person
1oz-25gm butter or margarine
1oz-25gm flour
3/4pt-400ml milk
1 tspn English mustard
8oz-225gm mature English cheddar cheese, grated
1 tomato per person for garnish
salt and pepper

1…Thoroughly clean the leeks. Retain as much of the green part as possible. Cut in half if very long. Steam the leeks until tender.
2…Wrap the slices of ham around the leeks and lay in individual gratin dishes
3…Melt the butter in a saucepan then add the flour. Cook for a couple of minutes but do not brown. Stirring all the time add the milk and simmer until a thick sauce develops. Add the mustard and 6oz-175gm of the cheddar. Cook until the cheese has melted. Season to taste then pour over the ham and leeks.
4…Slice the tomatoes and arrange on top. Sprinkle over the rest of the cheese. Place under a slow pre-heated grill and grill until golden brown and hot all the way through about 15 minutes.
Serve while piping hot and bubbling.

Chilli on Fire

Keep on going down the Roman Road and you will come to the place where this fiery dish is served!

1lb-450gm lean mince
2 onions finely sliced
2 cloves garlic crushed in a little salt
oil for frying
1 tin red kidney beans
1 tin Italian chopped tomatoes
2 tbls tomato puree
1/2 pt beef stock made with 1 whole stock cube
1 tspn hot chilli powder or two hot dried chillis
generous dash tabasco sauce
2 tspns mixed herbs
2 tspns mixed spices, eg, ginger, cumin, corriander, paprika
1 dssrtspn gravy granuels, more if necessary
salt and black pepper
Rice to serve

1...Heat the oil and fry the onions and garlic until golden brown. Add the minced meat and continue cooking over a high heat until the meat takes on a colour.
2...Add the chillis or powder, herbs and spices and cook for 2 minutes. Then add the tinned tomatoes, tomato puree, kidney beans and stock. Simmer gently for 35-40 minutes. Add more water or stock if necessary.
3...Sprinkle the gravy granuels over and stir into the chilli. Cook for about 10 minutes or until the chilli thickens.
4...Cook the rice in simmering water for 20 minutes. Strain and serve with the chilli. For a hotter chilli add more chilli powder at the beginning or tabasco sauce at the end.
Chilli can also be served with jacket potatoes and soured cream.

From the kitchen of...

GLENEAGLES
Butts Ash Lane. Dibden, Purlieu. Hants. Tel: 01703 842162
Proprietor: Geoff Mercer
Open: All day. 11am -11pm and Sunday 12 - 3pm and 7pm 10.30pm.
Children and casual callers welcome. Adventure playground for children. B.B.Q. Five **Real Ales**. Live Music every Wednesday. A popular pub with the locals.
Situated way off the beaten-track between Beaulieu river and Southampton water. Turn off the A326 and keep driving and you will find it at the bottom of an old Roman Road.

Forester's Burger

1lb-450gm shoulder of venison
4oz-110gm smoked streaky bacon
1 slice white bread
1 onion, chopped
1 or 2 cloves garlic
1 small egg
1 tbls brown sauce
generous pinch white pepper
salt

1...Dice the venison and then pass through a mincer or coarsely mince in the blender.

2...Fry the bacon until crisp. Cook the chopped onion in the bacon fat until golden.

3...Chop the cooked bacon and add with the onion to the minced venison.

4...Make fine crumbs from the slice of bread and add to the venison along with the beaten egg, brown sauce, salt and pepper. Mix well together then divide into eight portions.

5...Press the eight parts into burger shapes about 1/2inch-1cm thick and keep chilled until ready to grill or fry.

6...Grill or fry the burgers in oil for about 4 minutes each side. Longer for a well done burger.

To serve: Grill sesame buns (1 per burger) Put the burger inside and top with redcurrant jelly, or German mustard or grated Stilton cheese. Serve with red cabbage and celeriac slaw and pickled dill cucumbers.

Fish and Shellfish

Fish is highly nutritious and healthy as well as being low in saturated fats. When shopping always try to buy the whole fish rather than fillets or steaks. That way you can see what sort of condition it is in. Generally speaking, eyes should be bright and slightly protruding. The scales tend to come off ultra fresh fish easily. Its body should be firm, almost stiff, definitely not floppy. White fish should smell of the sea and not at all "fishy".

At home we tend to avoid serving fish both as a starter and main course, yet if you go to a seafood restaurant this is difficult to avoid. As long as the type of fish used and the sauce served have different characteristics, there's nothing wrong with serving fish twice.

Fillet of Salmon on a Bed of Spring Vegetables

A recipe taken from Mitchelin star chef, Ian McAndrew's book, A Feast of Fish.

4x 6oz-175gm filets of salmon
3oz-85gm each of mangetout, carrots, turnips, courgettes, calabrese,
French beans, cauliflower.
20 spring onions
1 tbls oil
2oz-50gm butter
salt and freshly ground white pepper
2fl oz-50ml Noilly Prat
300-450ml-1/2-3/4pt fish stock
juice of lemon

1...Prepare the vegetables as attractively as possible. Turn the courgettes into small barrels, pick the calabrese and cauliflower into small florets, choose small carrots and turnips and peel to preserve their original shapes. Blanch the vegetables separately and lightly. Refresh in iced water, then drain.
2...Season the salmon fillets. Heat the oil in the pan with half the butter and gently cook the fish for 3-4 minutes each side; be careful not to over-brown. Remove salmon from the pan and keep warm.
3...Tip off the excess fat from the pan and add the remaining butter. Toss the vegetables in this then season.
4...Add the Noilly Prat, fish stock and lemon juice. Bring to the boil and reduce the liquor slightly.
To serve:- Strain the vegetables from the liquor and arrange attractively on plates. Place the salmon in the centre and pour a little of the liquor over the vegetables and fish.

From the kitchen of...

THE BOAT HOUSE
Bar/Brasserie
Shamrock Way. Hythe Marina Village. Hythe. Tel: 01703 845594
Proprietors: Ian and Jane McAndrew
Chef: Ian McAndrew. Mitchelin Star. Cookery Writer.
Open: All year. Winter 11am - 3pm and 6am - 11pm. Longer hours during the summer months.
Booking advised in the brasserie but casual callers welcome if there's room. Children welcome. Most credit cards. Wheelchair access. Outside seating and River views. Seafood and Vegetarian Dishes. Outstanding food. Must not be missed.

Wild Avon Salmon

Wild salmon is normally associated with Scotland, yet the South of England has no problem belying this false impression.

The fishing is good. When the salmon makes its way, from March to September, to its spawning ground the river Avon is able to offer some of the best salmon fishing in the South of England. A 25lb catch is quite a regular occurrence.

Over the past ten years the National Rivers Authority have taken considerable action to improve the migration of salmon. The amount of catch has been restricted, particularly during the Spring running, fish to increase stocks and the river flow has been greatly improved. Fly fishing only, is allowed before May and the netting season is restricted to 15th April to 31st July.

Wild salmon is superior in flavour and texture compared with any farmed salmon, and although more expensive it is worth every penny.

It has been said that farmed salmon is so different from wild salmon that it shouldn't be called salmon at all. Nevertheless, farmed salmon for all its imperfections is cheap and nutritious, but is basically unsuitable for that truly special occasion.

Wild salmon is easy to recognize. It is long and thin like a sleek bullet, its jaw a ferocious, unfriendly opening. Its flesh is a firm muscle developed over the many hundreds of miles it has to swim, to reach its spawning ground. Its fins are well formed fans, inlaid with long sharp needles. It is a magnificent looking creature, quite unlike its flabby, commercial, brother.

Light Filo Scallop Shell

An elegant dish for two. Increase the quantities for a main course.

2 sheets filo pastry
4 fresh scallops in their shells
2oz-50gm wild mushrooms, sliced
1oz-25gm shallots, chopped
chopped fresh tarragon
1/4pt-150ml dry white wine
2 tbls dry sherry
1/4pt-150ml double cream
1/2pt fish stock
salt and pepper
1 egg, for egg wash and a knob of butter

1...Cut the scallops from their shells and slice in half. Clean the shells and lightly butter them.

2...Take one of the sheets of filo pastry and lightly egg wash. Place the second sheet of filo pastry on top and gently press together. Using a round cutter (approx 4"-9cm) and cut four rounds. Place into the scallop shells and press into the shape of the shell. Put to one side.

3...Saute the shallots and mushrooms for a few minutes in some butter. Add the chopped tarragon, white wine and sherry. Reduce by half. Add the fish stock and reduce again. Add the cream reduce again. This is the sauce for the scallops.

4...Place the scallop shells on a baking tray, then in a pre-heated oven, 200c/400f/gas 6 and bake for approx 5 minutes.

5...Saute the scallops in a little butter for 1 minute. Add the sauce, salt and pepper to taste.

6...Take two of the cooked scallop shells and place on two serving plates. Fill each one with the scallops in sauce. Then arrange the other shells on top.

From the menu of...

MONET'S BRASSERIE
Stanford Road. Lymington. Hants. Tel: 01590 672007
Proprietor: Mark Chandler
Chef: Edwin Whatley
Open: All year for Lunch and Dinner. Closed Monday. Open throughout the Christmas period.
Booking advised but casual callers welcome if there's room. Children welcome. Wheel chair access. Log fire in winter.
Seafood a speciality and all fresh fish is displayed in the restaurant.
New Wine Bar.

Baked Avon Salmon with Ginger Sauce

2lb-900gm fillet of salmon
salt and pepper
4 pinches Chinese five spice powder
4 knobs butter
4 sprigs of fresh fennel, dill or chervil
<u>Sauce</u>
1/4pt-150ml strong fish stock
1/4pt-150ml orange juice
1/4pt-150ml white wine
2 tbls white wine vinegar
1" piece of fresh ginger peeled and finely grated
2 tbls honey
1 tspn cornflour
4oz-110gm butter

1...First prepare the sauce. Place in a large heavy bottomed saucepan the fish stock, orange juice, white wine, wine vinegar, ginger and honey. Bring to the boil reduce the heat then simmer rapidly until reduce by half. Put to one side.
2...Remove the skin from the salmon fillet and cut into four portions. Grease a baking tray and lay on the salmon fillets. Smear a knob of butter on top of each fillet and lay on top the sprigs of chosen herb then sprinkle with the salt, pepper and Chinese five spice powder. Put in a pre-heated oven 220c/425f/gas7 and bake for 10 minutes.
3...Meanwhile re-heat the sauce. Mix the cornflour with a drop of water and add to the sauce. Simmer until the sauce thickens slightly. Then add the butter. Bring to a rapid boil.
4...Arrange the salmon fillets on warm plates and pour over some of the sauce. Serve with new potatoes, French beans and braised fennel.

Salmon Gratinee

A particular favourite of chef Simon, who often features this dish on his Sunday Lunch menu.

1lb.8oz-700gm fresh salmon fillet
4 egg yolks
2 tbls coarse mustard
1/2pt-275ml olive oil
generous amounts of fresh, finely chopped, tarragon, dill and basil.
salt and pepper

1...Cut the salmon fillet into four even sized pieces. Remove the skin.

2...Beat together the egg yolks, mustard and fresh herbs.

3...When mixed slowly whisk in the oil, as you would if making mayonnaise, until the mixture forms peaks (you may need more or less oil).

4...Spread the mixture evenly over the top of the salmon fillets and place on a well greased baking tray.

5...Place in a pre-heated oven 220c/425f/gas7 for 10 minutes. This is just the right amount of time for a juicy piece of salmon. Pre-heat a grill to very hot then remove the salmon from the oven and flash under the grill until the top is nicely browned. Keep your eyes on it as this will happen very quickly.

Serve with freshly cooked mange tout and minted new potatoes. Serves 4.

From the menu of...

MASTER BUILDERS HOUSE HOTEL
Bucklers Hard. Beaulieu. Hants. Tel: 01590 616253
Managers: Mr and Mrs C Plumpton
Chef: Simon Berry
Open: All Year including Christmas. PUB Winter 11am - 3pm and 6pm - 11pm. Summer open all day.
RESTAURANT 12noon - 2pm and 7pm - 9.30pm.
Children welcome. Wheelchair access. Credit cards accepted. Log Fires in Winter and outside seating with river views in Summer. Vegetarian dishes, seafood and local seasonal produce such as local game.
Recommended by Egon Ronay, Good Food Guide, AA Rosette.

Angling for a Fish

The River Avon runs along the length of the west side of the New Forest. It is nationally famous amongst coarse fishing enthusiasts. The river is well stocked with pike, grayling, barbel, chub, dace and roach. Weighty specimens of all these fish have been caught, giving the Avon the reputation of offering some of the best coarse fishing in the South of England.

It is a placid, meandering, river and a delightful place to fish. One of the best stretches for fishing is between Sopley and Winkton. At Sandle Heath, Allen's farm has four lakes where rainbow trout can be fished. By its side runs a woodland lined, stretch of the river Avon, where the more rare, brown trout can be caught. In other parts of the river it is still possible to gather a few crayfish, although most local crayfish are farmed.

On the eastern side of the Forest is the Beaulieu River. A popular river for sailors with a dream, but also excellent for coarse fishing. The eleven mile long river is well stocked right up to Bucklers Hard with perch/pike, bream, roach, tench and eel - some eel is commercially caught in traps.

With the exception of salmon and trout, most fresh water fish is relatively uncommon. The ferocious looking pike is probably one of the most popular, and prized in the chef's kitchen for the making of mousselines. Perch is similarly popular but is more bony. Grayling, which is related to the trout and of good flavour is almost never seen on a menu as is true of the golden barbel. Eel is better known but it is probably the conger eel that we are familiar with. Fresh water eel has a more dense, fatty flesh and can carry a robust sauce. Baby eels or elvers are delicious sauted or deep fried like whitebait. Bream and barbel are related to carp, but not so tasty, and do require a well seasoned, though not overly strong sauce.

If any of the fish mentioned above are featured on a restaurant menu, the chances are it has been locally caught.

Fresh Water Eels in Tomato Sauce

1lb.8oz-700gm fresh water eel. Skinned and cut into 2"-5cm
thick pieces
seasoned flour
oil for cooking
2 tins chopped Italian tomatoes or 1 tin a 8oz-225gm fresh
chopped tomato (skins removed)
1 tbls tomato puree
1 medium onion finely chopped
1 or 2 cloves garlic crushed
1 tbls dried herbs i.e. thyme, basil, tarragon or dill.
1/4pt-150ml dry white wine
1 tbls capers
salt and pepper

1...First make the sauce. Soften the onion in a little oil. Add the
crushed garlic and cook for 3 more minutes. Add the chopped
tomatoes, tomato puree, dried herbs, white wine and capers.
Simmer for about 20 minutes or until the sauce reduces and
thickens slightly.
2...Meanwhile toss the eel pieces in the seasoned flour. Heat some
oil in a frying pan and when hot quickly cook the fish until golden
all over.
3...Pour the sauce into the frying pan and simmer until the fish is
cooked. About 15 minutes (eel takes a little longer to cook than
most fish)
Serve with buttery ribbon noodles and green beans or calabrese.
Serves 4.

Meat, Poultry and Game

A menu is often designed around the meat or main course so this is probably the easiest dish to decide upon. It is best to make your choice depending upon seasonal availability. For example, game in the Autumn, poultry and pork at Christmas, lamb in Spring and early Summer, and beef, once the most popular of meats but less so now that red meat has lost favour with the healthies, is available all year round.

Meat is less fatty these days, which is a great shame since most of the flavour is carried in the fat. It is much better to eat and enjoy a good flavoursome, fatty, roast, but less often than you would a fatless, tasteless roast.

These days meat is sold ultra fresh, which invariably means it hasn't been hung unless it has been through the hands of a good traditional family butcher. Meat is hung to improve the flavour and tenderness.

Saute D'Agnueau Framboises

An exciting fruity lamb dish.

2lb-900gm lean lamb diced
8oz-225gm onion, chopped
oil for frying
2 bay leaves
bouquet garni
1/4pt-150ml raspberry vinegar
1pt-570ml stock
2 16oz tins raspberries in juice
1/2pt-275ml double cream
salt and pepper
freshly chopped parsley and coriander

1...Marinade the lamb in the vinegar for 2-3 hours.
2...Quickly fry the lamb in hot oil with the onion until the meat is brown.
3...Add the bay leaves, bouquet garni, stock and raspberries with their juice.
Bring to the boil.
4...Place in a covered casserole dish and cook in a moderate oven for approx
1 hour 30 minutes, or until the meat is tender. If the casserole dish isn't made
of metal turn the meat into a saucepan and return to the top of the stove. Put on
a high heat and reduce the liquid by approx half. Season to taste.
5...Add the cream and stir it through. Do not boil. Sprinkle with the freshly
chopped herbs and serve.

From the kitchen of...

NEW FOREST INN
Emery Down. Lyndhurst. Hants. Tel: 01703 282329
Proprietors: Michael Grove and Wendy Cole
Chef: Ray
Open: All year 11am - 11pm. Christmas day normal Sunday opening
Casual callers and well behaved children welcome. Credit cards accepted. Wheelchair access. Outside
seating and log fires in Winter. Food available all day including Sunday. Seafood and Vegetarian dishes.
Specialities such as Fresh Crab Thermidore and Fillet of Pork in Cashew Nut and Cream Sauce.

The Value of Meat

More than anything it is important to eat a balanced diet, yet because of the bad, sometimes uninformed publicity over recent years more people have ceased to eat meat - therefore, unbalancing their diet.

Meat is extremely good for you and meat products in general, such as milk and eggs are essential for a healthy diet. If you cut them out as vegans do then artificial substitutes have to be taken to replace lost nutriments.

Looking at it scientifically the body needs the building blocks of protein which are amino acids. The body is unable to manufacture these acids so it has to get them from 'high-quality' protein which is found in meat. Protein is essential to everyone but particularly to children who have fast growing bodies. The body also needs vitamin B12 and meat products are virtually the only dietary source: plant foods lack vitamin B12.

Minerals are also important. Iron, it is true is available in grains, nuts and pulses (via baked products) but by far the best source is meat, simply because it is chemically bound to the blood-protein haemoglobin and is therefore, rapidly absorbed into the blood. This is not the case with iron found in plants and lack of iron can cause anemia.

The amount of meat required for a healthy diet depends on whether you are male or female, a pregnant woman or a growing child, the last two. by the way need the most. The average person within these categories requires 6-9 oz of meat (or fish) per day. We are not talking 16oz T Bone steaks here but a few slices of roast beef or an average sized chicken breast.

Unbeknown to many people, most meat is reared in happy conditions. Fields full of cows (beef) and sheep (lamb) is proof of that, and in fact have always been reared that way; and these days it is not uncommon to see pigs rooting around in the open fields. Battery chicken do still exist and are very cheap, but for a little extra money you can easily purchase a free range chicken. The more of you that do, the more common and eventually cheaper free range chickens (and eggs) will become.

It is not in the farmer's interest not to look after his animals unless he wants to fork out money for hefty vets bills, and an animal that has been stressed in the slaughter house, as so many people claim, results in inedible meat, what's the point of that!

In the same way that a damaged apple is inedible so is damaged meat and great care is taken that this should not happen. At least the meat you eat has not been sprayed with insecticide and if an animal is ill the antibiotics it is given to help its recovery are no more harmful than the ones the doctor gives us to aid our own recovery.

Meat is essential for the development of strong healthy children and very important to people in active work, be it for pleasure or pay.

Braised Beef in Guinness with Colcannon and Carrots

One of Landlord Malcolm Frow's favourite dishes, which features regularly on his home-made specialities menu.

2lb-900gm chuck steak
1pt-570ml guinness
2 onions sliced
6 carrots sliced
1 tbls brown sugar
3 bay leaves
2 sprigs of thyme
handful chopped fresh parsley
freshly ground black pepper
1 tspn salt
1lb-450gm dried prunes
1oz-25gm cornflour mixed to a paste with cold water

1...Place all the ingredients except the cornflour in a casserole and marinate for 1-2 days.
2...Place on top of the stove and bring slowly to the boil. Skim frequently.
3...Cover and place in a warm oven. 170c/325f/gas3 for 2 hours to 2hrs 30 minutes or until the meat is tender.
4...Remove from the oven and add the cornflour mixture. Simmer on top of the stove for about 3 minutes until the sauce thickens.
5...Adjust seasoning and serve with colcannon and quartered boiled carrots. Serves 6.

Recipe for Colcannon on next page.

From the menu of...

THE FOREST HEATH RESTAURANT
Station Road. Sway. Hants. Tel: 01590 682287
Proprietor: Malcolm Frow
Chefs: Howard Triggs and Martin Thompson
Open: Winter, 11am - 3pm and 6pm - 11pm. Summer, 11am - 11pm. Saturday open all day throughout the year. Christmas Day open lunch time and evening.
Casual callers and children always welcome. Booking advised in restaurant but casual callers welcome if there's room. Credit cards accepted and wheelchair access. Log Fire and outside seating in large garden. Smoking and non-smoking restaurant. Children's special menu.
Traditional 2-Bar Village Inn with an excellent reputation for its home-made dishes and Own Real Ale. Accommodation. CAMRA (real ale) listed.

Colcannon

Malcolm Frow's recipe to go with his Braised Beef in Guinness. Colcannon is delicious served with many other dishes.

3lb-1.4kg scrubbed potatoes
1 medium head of cabbage, finely shredded
1 onion, finely chopped
1/2pt-275ml milk
salt and black pepper
4oz-110gm butter

1...Boil the potatoes until tender. Then drain and remove the skins.
2...Boil the shredded cabbage in a separate pan.
3...Gently cook the onion in the milk.
4...Mash the potatoes with the milk and onion then add the cooked cabbage and the butter. Mash well. Season with black pepper and salt and Serve.
Serves 6 people.

Fillet of Beef Carriages

2 6oz-175gm fillet steaks trimmed
4oz-110gm butter melted
2 tbls brandy
3oz-75gm stilton cheese cut into two slices
6x 8" sheets filo pastry
5 fl oz demi glace sauce (or a good brown gravy)
3 fl oz port wine
salt and freshly milled black pepper
watercress and radishes for garnish

1...Season the steak on both sides with salt and freshly milled pepper.
2...Heat 1oz-25gm of butter in a saute pan and seal steaks quickly on both sides then flame with the brandy. Remove from the pan and keep the pan juices for the sauce.
3...Take the sheets of filo pastry and brush with the melted butter, lay the sheets on top of one another at a 45degree angle to form two eight point stars.
4...Place a slice of stilton on top of each steak then wrap the steak in the filo pastry making a neat parcel. Brush all over with more butter.
5...Bake in a pre-heated oven 200c/400f/gas 6 for 15-20 minutes until golden and crispy.
6...To make the Port sauce: deglaze the saute pan with the Port wine. Then add the demi glace. Bring to the boil, correct the seasoning and pass through a fine chinois (sieve). Serve the steaks with the Port wine sauce and garnish with the watercress and radishes.
Serves 2.

From the menu of...

CARRIAGES RESTAURANT
At String of Horses
Mead End Road. Sway. Nr Lymington. Tel: 01590 682631
Proprietor: Mrs G.A. Reardon
Chef: Mr Julio Frias-Robles
Open: Wednesday - Saturday 7pm - 9pm and Sunday Luncheon 12.30 - 2pm
Booking essential in this non-smoking restaurant. Credit cards accepted
Seafood and vegetarian dishes. An intimate candlelit restaurant for romantic dining. A specially created a la carte menu served in sumptuous surroundings.

Pigs at Panage

The New Forest is in fact a large, open-plan farm yard. A farmer may only own a couple of acres of land, but the freedom of the Forest allows him to extend his husbandry far beyond those few acres.

In the middle ages half-wild pigs roamed the forests and could be extremely dangerous, particularly the boars. It would appear that little has changed. Today many domesticated pigs can be seen foraging in the forest; usually the British saddleback, which tend to enjoy the outdoor life.

Pigs at Pannage, as it is called, are eating acorns and beech mast that have fallen to The Forest floor. This is excellent food for pigs, although green acorns when eaten excessively by ponies and cattle can be poisonous. This right to pannage is called the Common-of-Mast.

At one time the pannage dates were fixed, from 25th September to 22nd November. However, sometimes the seasonal fall of nuts was late and hungry pigs had no qualms about invading local gardens, to supplement their diets on the tender crops. So, in 1964 an act was passed, whereby dates, after consultation with the Verderers*, could be varied. The commoners pay a small fee per animal to the Verderers.

There are also 3,500 acres of private commons where pannage laws are not kept, here local commoners can let their pigs roam throughout the year.

Pork reared in the open, with the freedom to forage has a stronger, tastier flavour and firmer texture than intensively reared pork.

* Verderers are part appointed, part elected people who are there to protect the rights and privileges of the commoners. The official Verderer is appointed by the Queen and presides over nine men. Five of them are commoners and are elected by commoners. It is largely an administrative post. They are given powers to pass by-laws pertaining to the welfare of The Forest.

Blanket of Pork with Capers and Paprika

1lb.8oz-700gm of pork shoulder, diced
2 small onions, finely sliced
1pt-570ml chicken stock
bouquet garni
2.1/2oz-60gm butter
2oz-50gm flour
1/4pt-150ml single cream
2 egg yolks
2 tbls paprika
1 tbls capers
1 red capsicum thinly sliced
1 tbls lemon juice
oil for frying
small amount of seasoned flour.

1...Toss the pork in the seasoned flour. Shake off the excess. Heat some oil in a frying pan and when hot lightly brown the pork pieces. Put to one side.
2...Melt the butter in a saucepan. Add the flour and paprika. Cook for a few minutes. Then pour in the chicken stock, stirring all the time until a sauce forms. Add the pork, bouquet garni, red capsicum and capers and simmer gently for about 1 hour. Or casserole in the oven. (Don't overcook or the meat will lose all of its flavour into the sauce).
3... When the pork is tender, add the cream. Heat through then add the egg yolks and lemon juice. Heat thoroughly but do not boil or the egg yolks will curdle.
4...Serve with basmati rice or new potatoes or even with a crust of puff pastry.

Chicken Korma

3lb-1.4kg boneless chicken, cubed
4 large onions, finely chopped
2 tbls ghee or unsalted butter
4 bay leaves
4-6 pieces of cardamon
1 piece cinnamon
1 tspn garlic, freshly ground
1 tspn ginger powder
1/2 tspn coriander powder
1/2 tspn salt
1 tbls white sugar
2 tbls plain yogurt
2 tbls almond powder
3 tbls coconut powder
1 tbls sultanas
1 tbls flaked almonds
1/2pt-275ml single cream

1...Heat the ghee or unsalted butter in a large saucepan and fry the onions until soft.
2... Add the chicken, bay leaves, cardamon, cinnamon, garlic, ginger and sugar. Cook on a moderate flame for approximately 15 minutes or until the chicken has cooked through.
3...Add all the other ingredients except the cream. Stir. Add the cream by pouring and stirring slowly. Put the lid on the saucepan and cook on a reduced flame for a further 5 minutes.
Serve with rice of your choice. Serves 6.

From the kitchen of...

Lions Court Supreme of Chicken

An exciting variation on a classic English dish, easy to prepare and beautifully presented. Breast of chicken filled with sage and onion, placed on a rosti and accompanied by delicious plain jus.

4 chicken supremes (breasts) with wing bone on
4oz-110gm sausage meat
1 medium onion
2 tbls fresh sage, chopped
4 tbls olive oil
2oz-50gm butter
milled black pepper
1pt-570ml chicken stock, fresh or stock cube
1 egg
2 medium potatoes
4fl oz-125ml white wine

1…Carefully scrape the meat away from the wing bone until it is clean. (Do not sever from the breast. Chop the knuckle of the end of this bone with a heavy knife so as not to splinter it. Reserve the meat from the wings for the stuffing.
2…Turn the chicken over so that the long fillet is showing. Remove this fillet and any sinew. Put to one side. Repeat this process with all the breasts.
3…Make a long slit/envelope (see illustration) where the fillet was, ready to take the stuffing.
4…Make the stuffing. Roughly chop the onion and put in a food processor with the sage, sausage and egg. Blend well until it forms a ball. Season with salt and milled black pepper.

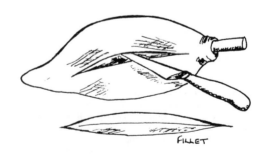

FILLET

5...Using a dessert spoon put some stuffing in each of the slits then close together. Then lay the fillet back over these two stuffed slits/envelopes.

6...Slowly heat a roasting tray with two tbls of olive oil. When hot place the chicken breasts uncut sides down in the oil to seal. When the meat turns white in colour turn over to seal the other side. Season with salt and milled black pepper and place in a pre-heated oven, 190c/375f/gas5 for approx 30 minutes.

7...Meanwhile make the rostis. Peel and de-eye the potatoes and place in a bowl of cold water. Then grate the potatoes on a coarse edged grater and place on a clean, flat, tea-towel. Roll up and squeeze the starch out.

8...Heat a pan, approx 6 minutes with a tspn of oil a 1oz-25gm butter. When the butter has melted sprinkle in some of the grated potato until the bottom of the pan is covered and the potato is about 1/2"-1cm thick. Press down with a slice. (You should get 2 rostis per potato) Keep the rest of the potato covered to prevent it browning. Cook for approx 2 minutes then turn over and cook the other side until golden brown on both sides. Turn out onto a pre-heated dinner plate and keep warm while you cook the three other rosti.

9...Remove the chicken from the oven and keep warm. Place the tray in which the chicken has been cooked on top of the stove over a high heat. Deglaze the pan with the white wine. Reduce by half. Pour in the chicken stock and bring to the boil (if you are using stock cubes thicken with 1 tspn of cornflour). If using homemade stock reduce by half until it naturally thickens. Adjust seasoning.

10...To serve: Place the rosti while on still on the plates under a grill to warm then arrange the chicken supreme on the rosti. Garnish with fresh sage leaves and serve the jus in a sauce boat.

From the kitchen of...

LIONS COURT RESTAURANT
29-31 High street. Fordingbridge. Hants. SP6 1AS
Tel: 01425 652006 Fax: 014525 657946
Proprietors: Michael and Jenny Eastick
Chef: Danny Wilson
Open: All year, including Christmas and New Year, except for two weeks January. Lunch 12 noon - 2pm.
Dinner 7pm until late. Small weddings and private parties welcome.
An excellent reputation for its A La Carte food, with 2 AA Rosettes. Restaurant has a relaxed atmosphere and serves food that favours fresh seasonal and local produce.
A charming 17th century, family run hotel and restaurant with delightful gardens running down to the River Avon.

Carib Chicken

4 supremes (breasts) of chicken, skinned
For the marinade
4 tbls white rum (i.e. Bacardi)
4 tbls molasses
2 fresh limes
For the sauce
1/2pt-275ml fresh apricot puree
1 tbls lime marmalade
4 fresh apricots or small tin of apricots
1 small fresh mango
To serve
Cook enough rice for 4 people then add to it sliced mushrooms,
chopped shallot or onion, diced red pepper, baby sweet corn and any
other vegetable of your choice..

1...Place the chicken pieces in a shallow glass or china dish.
2...Mix together the molasses, the rum and the juice and finely shredded rind of the limes. Pour over the chicken, cover and leave in the fridge to marinate for 24-48 hours. Turn the chicken occasionally to ensure an even marinade.
3...Mix together the apricot puree the lime marmalade, the sliced apricots and half the mango cubed or sliced. Remove the chicken from the marinade and add the marinade to the sauce. Gently heat through and keep warm.
4...Lightly oil a heavy bottomed or preferably non-stick frying pan and saute the chicken. Turn frequently to prevent the molasses burning. When the chicken is sealed on both sides cover with a lid, reduce the heat to low and cook until the chicken is done.
5...To serve. Place the chicken breasts on beds of vegetable rice. Pour over the sauce and garnish with slices of the remaining half of mango.

N.B. If apricots are out of season, most supermarkets sell a fruit compote called Bon Maman which makes an ideal alternative.
From the menu of...

THE JOLLY SAILOR
Victoria Quay. Ashlett Creek. Fawley. Hants. Tel: 01703 891305
Proprietors: Tony and Sue Redfern.
Open: Winter - All day opening Friday and Saturday. Summer All day opening every weekday.
Children and dogs are welcome and wheelchairs are easily accommodated.
A wide-spread reputation has grown for their good food in both the two bars and restaurant. Delicious Roast Carvery is served on Sunday from October to May. Friendly, welcoming surroundings decorated with many nautical themes. Gentle live music played Friday and Sunday. Real Ales on tap. The picnic tables outside overlooks the yacht club and the many boats of visiting yachtsmen.

Commoner's Rights

The Hampshire Basin, where the New Forest resides is largely infertile. The soil is thin and underneath lies, chalk, gravel, and clay, hence most farming is given over to livestock, cattle, pigs and ponies.

The rights of the commoner were established almost by default in the time of William the Conqueror. Before his time the farmers enclosed their land and farmed in the normal way. When William came along with his interest in deer hunting he ordered that all fences be removed to allow a free run across the land. In recompense the farmers were given common rights and allowed to let their livestock wander freely through The Forest. This right was withdrawn during June and July when the fawns were born and from the end of November to the beginning of May when natural food was scarce and all that was available must go to the deer. Not the most generous of recompenses and was the cause of tremendous hardship to the commoners.

Over the centuries rights and uses of the Forest have changed and in 1851 an Act of Parliament was passed where in return for the foresters agreeing to allow 10,000 acres of open land to be fenced off for timber production they were allowed the common use of the forest for 365 days of the year.

The rights of the Commoner are not available to everyone and anyone. Only to those with property and land in The Forest, albeit in some cases a small front garden and they must hold at least one of the five "common rights" to farm The Forest.

These Common rights are-: Common of Mast: the right to turn pigs on the Forest. Common of Turbary: the right to cut turf. Common of Fuelwood: eighty Commoners are allowed to use the wood cut by the Forestry Commission for firewood in the house. Common of Marl: An almost obsolete right. The gathering of marl for spreading as manure on Commoner's land.

The "Swan's" special Duck-Pot

A hearty, warming dish, excellent sustenance after a long walk in the Forest.

5/6lb-2.5/3kilos duck (preferably Barbary)
2lb-900gm smoked back bacon, de-rinded and cut into lardons
1lb.8oz-700gm good quality pork sausages
8oz-225gm tinned plum tomatoes
1lb-450gm tinned flagelot beans
4-5 tbls tomato puree
1 tspn olive oil
1/2pt-275ml dry, 'heavy' red wine i.e Cabernet Sauvignon
1pt-570ml ham stock (bullion paste now available in most good
supermarkets)
1lb-450gm shallots
8 sprigs of fresh thyme
2oz-50gm fresh 'flat leaf' parsley, stalks removed
4 sprigs of fresh sage
10! whole cloves of fresh garlic, crushed

1...Remove wings from duck and discard. Cut legs from duck and cut
remaining carcass into 6 pieces. With a fork prick the skin of the duck and the
pork sausages. Rub salt and pepper onto the duck and place in a shallow dish
with the sausages. Pour over the red wine and add 2 sprigs of thyme. Cover
with film and leave in the fridge overnight to marinade.
2...The next day heat a large frying pan with the olive oil and add duck
pieces, quickly sealing the skin. Reduce heat to medium and add the sausages.
Reserve the wine marinade. When the duck pieces are golden in colour and
the sausages are cooked through, remove from the pan and place in a large
casserole dish.

cont'd

3...Drain away three quarters of the fat from the pan,(keep the fat, it's excellent to use for delicious fried breakfast). Add the whole peeled shallots and lardons of bacon to the pan and gently cook over a low heat. Add the crushed garlic just before the shallots turn golden-brown in colour. Once cooked add to the casserole dish.

4...In a large saucepan pour the plum tomatoes and juices, the flagelot beans, tomato puree, red wine marinade, remaining thyme and fresh sage. Stir together and gently heat through. Pour this over the cooked meats in the casserole dish. Add enough ham stock to just cover the mixture.

5...Cover the casserole with a tight fitting lid and place in a pre-heated oven 190c/375f/gas5 for 1hr-1hr 30 minutes or until the duck is falling off the bone.

6...Check the casserole after 45 minutes and if it seems too dry, add more stock. Add the parsley leaves about 10 minutes before the end of cooking. Adjust seasoning.

7...Serve piping hot with sauted potatoes and lots of garlic bread to mop up the juices. Serves 6-10 depending on appetite!!

From the Kitchen of...

THE SWAN INN
Wayside Inn
Swan Green. Lyndhurst. Hants. Tel: 01703 282203
Managers: Martin and Clare Burr
Supervisory Chef: Martin Burr
Open: All year 11am - 11pm. Mon - Sat, 12noon - 10.30pm Sunday.
Casual callers and children especially welcome. Mini Pet-Farm in garden. Dogs welcome in the bar.
Booking advised for meals. Credit cards accepted. Wheelchair access. Baby changing facilities. Log fires in Winter and outside seating in Summer. Vegetarian dishes and specialities such as home-made pies and game dishes.

Marinated Duck

Breast of New Forest duck marinated in French mustard and honey

2 duck breasts
2 tbls French mustard
4 tbls clear honey
3 tbls olive oil
2 tbls peanut oil (for cooking)
1 orange
salt and pepper

1...Prepare the duck breast by removing excess fat and removing the sinew from the fillet.
2...Finely grate the zest from the orange.
3...Squeeze the juice of the orange into a metal bowl. Add the French mustard, honey, olive oil, orange zest, salt and pepper and mix together.
4...Place the duck breasts into the marinade and leave for 6-12 hours in the refrigerator.
5...Remove the duck breasts from the marinade. Put the peanut oil into a saute pan (use a pan that can be transferred to the oven). Place the duck breasts skin down into the hot peanut oil. Cook until golden brown. Turn over the breasts and place in a moderate oven 200c/400f/gas6 for 8-9 minutes. Take from the oven and rest for 10 minutes.
6...Take a little of the marinade and warm in a saucepan. Slice the duck breasts. Pour some sauce on to hot dinner plates and arrange the duck slices on top. Serves 2.

From the menu of...

MONTAGU ARMS HOTEL
Place Lane. Beaulieu. Hants. Tel: 01590 612324
Proprietors: Mr and Mrs P Leach
Chef: Simon Fennell
Open: All year. In the Pub, restaurant and Hotel.
Casual callers and children welcome. Credit cards accepted. Log fires in Winter and outside seating in Summer. Vegetarian dishes and home-made speciality breads i.e. onion, raisin, walnut, sun dried tomato, olive and mixed spice.

Brace of Quail Stuffed with Spinach and Mushrooms

8 whole quail
4oz-110gm spinach
4oz-110gm button mushrooms
1oz-25gm breadcrumbs
1 glass red wine and half glass port
1/2oz-10gm tomato puree
1lb-450gm shallots
2oz-50gm brown sugar
1/2pt-275ml stock, made from the quail bones
mixed herbs, fresh
butter and salt and pepper

1...Very carefully take out the bones from the quails. A fiddley job but worth it. Use the carcasses for the stock.
2...Chop up the mushrooms and two of the shallots.
3...Cook the spinach in a very small amount of water with a pinch of salt. When cooked chop it up and add to the shallots and mushrooms. Put this mixture in a pan with some butter and saute off. Add the breadcrumbs and season.
5...Stuff the quails with this mixture and place in a roasting tin in the oven 190c/375f/gas5 for 15 minutes.
6...When the quails are cooked remove them from the pan and keep warm.
7...Put the pan with the quail juices on a high heat on top of the stove and add the red wine and the port. Cook for about 1 minute and then add the tomato puree and brown sugar. Cook until the sauce thickens.
8...Add the whole peeled shallots, then the chicken stock and a few mixed herbs. Simmer rapidly until the sauce coats the back of a spoon and has a sheen.
9...Place two quails on each hot dinner plate. Surround with the shallots and pour the sauce over. Garnish with more mixed herbs. Serves 4.

From the kitchen of...

TOAD HALL RESTAURANT
The Cross. Burley. Hants. Tel: 01425 403448
Proprietor: Mrs C Flower
Chef: Mr May
Open: All year. In the heart of the Forest. A perfect retreat in a beautiful, true, Victorian Country House Hotel and restaurant. Specialising in seafood, steaks and game.

Pheasant in Apple and Celery Sauce

brace of pheasants (jointed, breast bone left on)
2 bay leaves
1/2oz-10gm parsley
8oz-225gm onion, finely chopped
12oz-350gm celery finely chopped (reserve leaves for garnish)
6 bramley apples, peeled, cored and finely chopped
6oz-175gm butter
4oz-110gm plain flour
16 fl oz dry cider
6fl oz double cream
salt and pepper
2 dessert apples, cored, sliced into rings and sauted in butter

1…Make the stock. Put the pheasant carcasses, bay leaves and parsley in 2pts-570ml water. Bring to the boils and simmer for 20-30 minutes.
2…Coat the pheasant joints in flour and fry until the outside is sealed and golden coloured. Place in a casserole dish.
3…Sweat the onions and celery in the butter until opaque. About 5 minutes. Add the bramley apples and cook for a further 5 minutes.
4…Remove from the heat and add the flour to absorb the fat. Stir in. Return to the heat and stir in the cider and stock. Bring to the boil. Pour this sauce over the pheasants. Cover and place in a medium oven for 45 minutes.
5…Remove the pheasant and keep warm. Pour the sauce into a saucepan and bring to the boil. Add the cream and season to taste.
6…Arrange a leg and a breast on each plate. Pour over the sauce and garnish with the apple rings and celery leaves.
Serve with baby new potatoes and fresh seasonal vegetables. Serves 4.

From the kitchen of…

THE GEORGE INN
Wayside Inn
Bridge Street. Fordingbridge. Hants. Tel: 01425 652040
Managers: Geoff and Jackie Lawson.
Chefs: Dave and Annmarie
Open: All year. 11am - 11pm. Closed Christmas night. Credit cards accepted.
Outside seating. Delicious home-made vegetarian dishes a speciality.
A Wayside Inn in a stunning position on the River Avon where their friendly staff are waiting to welcome you. Home cooked meals, fine ales and soft drinks are available all day for all the family.

Royal Venison

The New Forest was the last of the Royal Hunting grounds. William the Conqueror in the early 9th Century set aside the New Forest region specifically for the preservation of its deer purely to satisfy his hunting pleasures. He called it the New Forest, "His New Forest".

He completely disregarded the rights of the local forest people and over-rode their laws with laws of his own to protect his precious deer. These laws proved to be a huge restriction on farming and crofting activities and the cause of much hardship. The farmers weren't even allowed to protect what land they already had. Fences had to come down so that William could hunt unhindered and of course the indiscriminate deer had no problem consuming the farmer's crops.

As was expected, the deer were stripping the forest of its trees and in the late thirteenth century a tree-growing act was passed.

Over the centuries the Royal hunting rights have diminished and after the reign of James II there are no records of Royals exercising their hunting rights. This proved good news for the Commoner's and bad news for the deer, for in 1850 the Deer Removal Act was passed thus allowing the outright destruction of the deer and the re-development of land enclosures. Not all the deer were eradicated. Some found bolt holes in the denser, more remote parts of The Forest and gradually their numbers increased.

There are currently five different species of deer roaming The Forest floor, and their numbers (around 1,500) are today kept in check to protect farmers crops by annual culling. Forest keepers are highly skilled in the use of high powered rifles and their culling activities are usually of sick, weak, and old animals.

At Bolderwood there is a deer sanctuary where deer can come and go as they please. The deer are fed to encourage them there. There is also room for the public to view them.

Red deer, the largest species in the country and fallow deer are the ones most commonly seen, probably because they live in large herds. Roe deer live in small family groups, usually the buck, doe and one or two fawns. You might be lucky to see them at dawn or dusk. The sika deer was introduced from Japan and can sometimes be seen in the Brockenhurst area. The muntjac deer is the rarest of them all. This tiny asian species is usually well hidden under thick woodland growth. Most deer are culled from September to February. This is the Venison Season.

Venison is a popular meat and features on many New Forest menus. A gourmet trip to the new Forest is seriously missing something if a sample of venison is not taken at least once during your stay.

Ragout of Venison with Caramelised Apple

1lb.8oz-700gm diced shoulder of venison, 1/2"cubes
2oz-50gm seasoned flour
1oz-25gm butter and 2 tbls vegetable oil
2 carrots, cut into 1/4" lengths then sliced
1 medium onion, peeled and diced
1 tbls tomato paste
1/2pt-275ml beef stock
1/2pt-275ml dry red wine
1 tbls red wine vinegar
8 juniper berries and bouquet garni
2oz-50gm redcurrant jelly
2 medium apples and 1oz-25gm demerara sugar

1...Toss the venison in seasoned flour. Shake off the excess.
2...In a large frying pan heat the butter and oil and quickly fry the venison until browned on all sides. Transfer to a large oven-proof casserole. In the remaining fat fry the carrots and onions until golden. Transfer to the casserole.
3...Stir the remaining flour into the residual fat in the frying pan. Fry until brown. Remove from the heat and gradually add the stock, red wine and red wine vinegar, half the redcurrant jelly and the tomato paste. Bring to the boil, stirring all the time. Pour the sauce over the casserole. Add the bouquet garni and juniper berries. Season to taste.
4...Cover the casserole and cook in a pre-heated oven 170c/325f/gas3 for 2hrs 15 minutes to 2hrs 30 minutes until the meat is tender. Remove bouquet garni.
5...Cut the apples in half across their 'tummys' and scoop out the cores and pips so that a hollow is formed. Brush liberally with melted butter and sprinkle over the demerara sugar. Grill until the sugar has melted and caramelised to a golden hue. Fill the centre with the remaining redcurrant jelly and serve with the Venison ragout. Delicious with creamed potatoes or buttered noodles. Serves 4.

From the menu of...

BALMER LAWN HOTEL AND RESTAURANT
Lyndhurst Road. Brockenhurst. Hants. Tel: 01590 623116
Proprietor: Hilton Associate Hotel
Chef: Norman Dunford
Open: Restaurant, all year. 12.30 - 1.45 and 7pm - 9.30pm.
Casual callers and children welcome. Credit cards accepted. Wheelchair access. Vegetarian Dishes.
Lounge and bar snacks available and traditional roast Sunday lunch.

Forest Vines

If you are as interested in the production of wine as you are in drinking it then Lymington vineyard is the place for you.

The six acres of vineyards at Lymington were planted in 1979. A variety of vines have been planted in order to produce a single grape variety wine or a blended wine, depending upon how the ripening season has gone. The site of the vineyard is only 50ft above sea level and is well suited for growing vines. It is well sheltered and the growing season is lengthened by the light reflected from the sea.

Visitors can see all stages of wine production from the growing of the grapes when the buds begin to form in May to the actual making of the wine when the grapes are picked depending on ripeness in October.

Lymington Wine Ham

4lb-1.8kg gammon ham
1 bottle Lymington, dry white wine
8oz-225gm green grapes, peeled
squeeze of lemon juice
2 medium onions, skinned
2 carrots, scrubbed
1 tspn cloves
1 tspn fennel seeds
1 tspn black peppercorns
few sprigs thyme
1 tbls corn flour
2 tbls cream

1...Put the gammon in a large saucepan with cold water. Place over a medium heat and bring to the boil. Remove from the heat a strain off the water. This preparation removes excess salt and scum.

2... Rinse out the saucepan and put the gammon back in with the white wine, onions, carrots, cloves, fennel, peppercorns and thyme. Bring to the boil then reduce the heat. Cover the saucepan and simmer gently for 1hr 30 minutes or until the ham is tender.

3...Remove the ham and keep warm. Strain the wine flavoured stock and put in a clean saucepan. Peel the grapes and squeeze over the lemon juice to prevent them going brown. Mix the cornflour with a drop of water and add to the stock. Stir over a gentle heat until the sauce thickens. Add the cream and the peeled grapes. Simmer for a few minutes until the grapes are heated through but don't over cook otherwise the grapes will loose their texture.

4...Carve thick slices of ham pour over some of the sauce. Serve with new potatoes and green beans or spring cabbage.

Puddings
and
Desserts

Tastes in puddings vary considerably. Some prefer something cool and refreshing or juicy and fruity and others prefer to indulge in something rich and gooey or creamy and moussy.

Choice of dessert is best dependent on what has gone before. Serve something light if the main meal has been rich and vice-versa. Avoid serving pastry or cream if either of these two ingredients have been involved in the starter or main dish. And again, avoid a fruit pudding if fruit has been involved in an earlier dish. These simple rules will ensure a balanced and interesting meal.

Autumn Forest Fruits

There is a certain charm to gathering the autumnal fruits of the New Forest not to be experienced anywhere else - for you are not alone!

While you are picking, amongst other things, ripe juicy blackberries the ponies, deer and other furry forest creatures are picking their own favourite crop. This theraputic mingling with The Forest's fortune, our four legged friends, the sharing of their space is a gift we can treasure within our memory for us long as we live.

Autumn is the natural time for most wild fruits to come to fruition, and you can walk the leaf strewn footpaths and bridleways and bag your free food. Blackberries are trickily abundant, sloes are blooming with their tarty, ripeness and rose hips wave beyond the normal reach. In the broadleaved parts of The Forest a search should reward you with sweet chestnuts, cobnuts and crab apples.

The fun doesn't end with the gathering either, for much pleasure is ultimately gained by the preservation of your efforts. The turning of your crops into glistening chutneys, jams, jellies and fruit wines.

With the exception of blackberries, hedgerow fruits are extremely sour, they therefore require considerably more sugar than normal, cultivated fruit. However, because of their high pectin content hedgerow fruits are excellent for making Victorian style fruit jellies that are traditionally served with meat and game.

Apple and Blackberry Sorbet

A simple dish to serve either between courses or as a refreshing dessert after a robust Autumn dinner.

1 large cooking apple
8oz-225gm blackberries
8oz-225gm granulated sugar
1/2pt-275ml water
1 tspn lemon juice
2 egg whites

1...Put the sugar and water in a saucepan. Heat gently until the sugar dissolves then boil rapidly for 8 minutes.
2...Peel, core and slice the apple. Wash and dry the blackberries. Add the sugar syrup and simmer the fruit until the apple has collapsed.
3...Blend the fruit to a smooth puree and pass through a fine sieve.
Return the fruit puree to a clean sauce pan and bring to the boil. Boil for 5 minutes
4...Meanwhile put the egg whites in a clean bowl and whisk to soft peaks. While the beaters are still turning slowly pour in the boiling fruit puree. Continue beating until the mixture bulks out and cools.
5...Pour into a plastic container and place on the lid. When the mixture is almost cold put in the freezer and freeze on high for at least 10 hours.

Self Pick Farms

What a wonderful concept the self-pick farm was. In its early days there was a clamour of excited voices praising the farms who opened their gates to the general public so that they could search among the brown earth rows for a choice cabbage, the best beans, the finest fruits... Customers could experience the thrill of picking something straight from the ground without having to grow it first. But the greatest advantage of all was the value, everything was cheaper, not only cheaper than the shops but cheaper than growing it yourself.

The emphasis on the self-pick expedition has changed slightly and is now more often than not considered part of a family day out. There are few simple, inexpensive pleasures left, yet to be out in the warm English sun harvesting a punnet of ripe juicy strawberries or perhaps ruby red raspberries, maybe both, knowing that you will soon be consuming them with some real dairy ice cream or perhaps a spoonful of thick, buttery, clotted cream.

If you are picking quantities to make jam, why not take the whole family and have a competition, who can pick the most in the shortest time, or who picks the best looking punnet, the prize? the biggest dish of strawberries for tea.

In some instances the Farm Shop has become a by-product of the self-pick farm. Here you can buy for a small extra premium, the freshly gathered crops already picked for you.

Farm Shops have developed considerably over the years. A lot of fun can be gained by venturing down dusty farm tracks in search of these, often barn converted, shops. A chance to see the workings of the farmyard and often a delight for children if the is some livestock to see - and much more than vegetables can now be bought. Many farms have gone into producing their own ice-creams, yogurts, sausages, jams and much, much, more, from the produce and livestock on their farm.

There is a self-pick farm and farm shop at Hazelcopse Farm at Beaulieu.

P.Y.O. Pudding

This recipe makes the most of the soft fruits available to pick at Hazelcopse, together with delicious bread from the bakery.

2lb-900gm mixed soft fruits, i.e. strawberries, raspberries, redcurrants, blackcurrants (P.Y.O or from the farm shop)
8oz-225gm castor sugar
thin slices of Hazelcopse bakery white bread, crusts removed
thick cream to serve (available from farm shop)

1...Mix together the fruit and sugar in a large non-metalic bowl and leave to stand overnight.
2...Lightly grease a 1.3/4pt-1litre ceramic pudding basin.
3...Cut a circular slice of bread to fit the bottom of the basin. Cut most of the remaining bread into wedges and use to line the sides of the basin.
4...Put the fruit into a saucepan and bring gently to the boil then simmer for 2-3 minutes or until the fruit just softens. Cool slightly.
5...Pour half the fruit into the bread lined basin then place a slice of bread on top. Add the remaining fruit and juice, but save a little of the juice for serving.
6...Place one or two slices of bread on top of the pudding to make a lid. Cover with a plate just large enough to fit on top and weigh down. Refrigerate for at least 10 hours.
7...Loosen the pudding by running a knife around the edge. Place a serving dish on top of the basin. Invert the whole thing quickly and remove the basin. If the bread is not soaked through pour over the reserved juice. Cut the pudding into large wedges and serve with thick dollops of cream.

Recipe supplied by...

HAZELCOPSE FARM
P.Y.O., Farm Shop and Bakery
Hatchet Lane. Beaulieu. Hants. Tel: 01590 612696
Proprietor: Messrs Dolbear
Open: Bakery and Farm Shop all year, 7 days /wk 8.30 am - 5.30pm.
P.Y.O. from June onwards. 8.30am - 6.30pm
Credit cards Accepted and children welcome.
All soft fruits and much more available on the P.Y.O. and freshly baked bread, home baked cakes and savouries in the bakery.

Upside-down Apple and Cider Tart

New Forest farmhouse cider is still made at Burley in the old fashioned way. At the turn of the century it was made by Eli Sim's cider press. Today it is produced from local orchard apples and cider fruit and can be bought at the Commoner's Forest holding where it is sold straight from the barrel.

1/2 pt-275ml sweet cider
5 cox dessert apples
4oz-110gm castor sugar
2oz-50gm butter
finely grated rind of half a lemon

3oz-75gm plain flour
3oz-75gm ground almonds
4oz-110gm butter
1 tbls icing sugar
pinch of salt
1 small beaten egg

1...Peel the apples. Cut into quarters and remove the core. Cover and put to one side.
2...In a shallow, metal, saute or frying pan (must have a metal handle) put the butter and sugar. Place over a gentle heat until the butter has melted and the sugar dissolved. Raise the heat and cook until the sugar and butter begins to turn golden. Now add the cider. The mixture will bubble up. Lower the heat slightly and simmer until the sauce reduces by half.
3...Add the apples and lemon rind and simmer for five minutes until the apples are coated and golden. Move the apples around the pan to form a pattern. Put to one side.
4...Mix the flour and ground almonds together and rub in the butter. When you have fine bread crumbs add the icing sugar.
5...Beat the egg and use to bind the mixture together. Rest the pastry for 20 minutes in the fridge.
6...Roll out the pastry to about an inch larger than the pan. Lay the pastry on top of the apples and tuck the edges in.
7...Bake in a pre-heated oven. 220c/425f/gas7 for 25-30 minutes. Remove from the oven and turn upside down immediately onto its serving plate. But do not remove the pan. Let stand in a warm place for twenty minutes. Serve warm with whipped cream that has been dredged with molasses sugar.
Serves 4.

Gooseberry and Eldeflower Crush

Measurments don't have to be strictly acurate for this very simple dessert. When gathering your elderflowers choose umbels that have only just opened.

1lb gooseberries
4 or 5 heads (umbels) of elderflowers
4oz-110gm castor sugar
4 or 5 broken meringue shells
1pt-570ml double cream

1...Wash and then top and tail the gooseberries. Place in a saucepan with the sugar and elderflowers. Add about 3 tbls water. Cover and simmer gently until the gooseberries are tender and the sugar has dissolved. Stand until cold.
2...Remove the elderflowers heads from the gooseberries (don't worry if a few petals get left behind).
3...Put the gooseberries with the cream in either 1)a blender for a smooth mixture 2) a mixer for a more textured mixture. Blend or beat together until the mixutre thickens. Add more cream if too runny. (Be careful not to over beat)
4...Fold in the roughly broken meringues. Spoon into glass dishes and serve with hazelnut shortbread.
Serves 4-6.

White Chocolate Truffle Cake
and Coffee Cream

Forget your diet for this pud!

The Cake
7.1/2oz-210gm self-raising flour
1/2oz cocoa powder
6oz-175gm castor sugar
6oz-175gm butter
2 eggs beaten
milk, enough for dropping consistency
few drops vanilla essence
The Filling
16oz-450gm rich white chocolate
16fl oz double cream

The Coffee cream:- 1/2pt275ml double cream, 1oz-25gm brown sugar,
2 tspns granulated sugar.

Brandy or Port (optional)

1...First make the sponge. Set oven to 180c/350f/gas4, and line and grease a
8" cake tin.
2...Cream the butter and castor sugar together until pale and light.
3...Add the beaten eggs, beating constantly until snowy.
4...Sift together the flour and cocoa and fold into the mixture, then add the
vanilla essence and a drop of milk to form a dropping consistency. Spoon into
the prepared cake tin and bake for approx 1 hour 30 minutes. When cooked
place on a wire rack to cool. Cut the cake into three or four rounds. Only one
is required for this recipe. Individually wrap and freeze the ones you don't
use.
5...Next prepare the filling. Break the chocolate into a basin and put the basin
over a saucepan of boiling water. (It is essential no moisture gets into the
chocolate) When the chocolate has melted cool slightly.
6...Whisk the double cream until it forms a soft peak/ribbon.
7...The Coffee Cream: gently heat the cream and sugar to blood heat.
Sprinkle the granulated coffee into the cream and stir until dissolved.
8...To assemble. Line the base of an 8" loose bottomed cake tin with
greaseproof paper. Put a cake round in the bottom. Sprinkle with the brandy
or port.

cont'd

9...Gently and thoroughly whisk half the melted chocolate into the cream then fold in the remaining chocolate. Pour over the cake base and cover closely with cling film or a circle of greaseproof to remove the air. Refrigerate for about 6 hours until the mixture has set.

10...Run a knife dipped in hot water around the edge of the cake to loosen then place on a plain plate. Dust the top liberally with cocoa. Serve small wedges of this rich dessert with fresh strawberries, slices of Kiwi, peeled grapes and the coffee cream.

N.B. This cake will serve about 12 people. It freezes well.

From the kitchen of...

Hazelnut Meringue Roulade with Toffee Cream

4 large egg whites
8oz-225gm castor sugar
1 tbls cornflour
1 tspn vanilla essence
1 tspn vinegar
2oz-50gm ground roasted hazelnuts
1/2pt-275ml double cream
Toffee sauce
3oz-75gm brown sugar
2oz-50gm butter
3 tbls double cream
Equipment - 12" x 15" metal tray and a sheet of baking parchment

1...First make the toffee sauce. Put all the sauce ingredients into a saucepan over a gentle heat and stir until the sugar has dissolved. Bring to the boil and boil for 5 minutes. Cool.

2...Whisk the egg whites until stiff. Whilst whisking add the cornflour, vinegar, vanilla and castor sugar.

3...Once these have combined to make a firm meringue mix carefully <u>fold</u> in the ground hazelnuts.

4...Spread evenly over the parchment lined baking tray and place in a pre-heated oven 140c/275f/gas1 for 15 - 20 minutes (the meringue must not be dried out in the traditional way)

5...Meanwhile lay out a second piece of parchment on to a flat surface. Turn out the meringue while still warm on to this sheet and roll up.

6...When cool, whip the cream to soft peaks and add the toffee sauce. Un-roll the meringue and spread the toffee flavoured cream evenly over the surface. Re-roll (don't worry if it cracks it adds to the appearance) chill until required. Delicious served with fresh raspberries.

From the kitchen of...

JJ'S DESSERTS
Unit 13. Netley Marsh Workshops. Ringwood Rd. Netley Marsh. Hants.
Tel: 01703 660814 Fax: 01703 667311
Proprietor/Chef: Jeni Scholfield
Freelance caterer. A small company specialising in made-to-order desserts for restaurants and private catering. They also undertake other outside catering. Functions for up to 50 persons and executive/business luncheons.

Afternoon Tea

Afternoon tea abounds in the New Forest. From three thirty onwards tearooms and cafes are filled with the mellifluous sound of teaspoons tinkling against the side of tea cups; and the gentle consumption of home-made cakes, freshly baked scones and little dishes of cream, heralds a satisfying end to a fun filled day.

Lemon Rock Cakes

A simple recipe that is often forgotten.

1lb-450gm self-raising flour
8oz-225gm butter
8oz-225gm mixed fruit
6oz-175gm castor sugar
few drops lemon essence
pinch of salt
1 egg
milk for binding
glace cherries for decoration

1...Mix the salt into the flour. Cut the butter into cubes and rub into the flour to form a crumble consistency.
2...Add the sugar and dried fruit and mix well.
3...Beat the egg with about 2 tbls milk and the lemon essence. Add to the crumb mixture and bind together to a stiff dough with a fork.
4...Grease 2 baking sheets and spoon the mixture onto the sheet in rough rounds to resemble rocks. Top each one with half a glace cherry. Bake in a pre-heated oven 180c/350f.gas4 for approx 20 minutes or until golden. Place on a rack to cool and sprinkle with castor sugar. Makes about 14 cakes.

Let's Bake a Cake

It is a great sadness that the weekly tradition of baking a cake has drifted away. Yet the large display of cakes on supermarket shelves and the number of cake shops and patisseries around, and, the number of people who frequent local tea-rooms for a cup of tea and a piece of cake, suggests the tradition of eating cake is very much with us.

Lack of time, for so many women, the usual baker of cakes, is probably the main reason for the demise of the home-baked cake.

Cake is often viewed as something special, a marker for a that personal event like a birthday, a wedding, a christening, a retirement or an anniversary. Also, universally it is made to represent religious festivals such as Christmas and Easter.

Cake making isn't at all difficult, in fact it is difficult to go wrong, provided you follow the instructions to the letter. The most important rule is, always measure your ingredients. Unless you make cakes on a regular basis, (and even then lack of concentration can result in a flop) don't be tempted to guess the measurements. The smallest discrepancy can give imperfect results. Secondly, cake mixtures should be treated with respect. The aim is to get as much air into the mixture as possible, then keep it there. In other words once the beating, whisking or creaming is complete the dry ingredients should be carefully folded in.

Here are a few extra tips. 1. Use soft margarine or make sure the butter is very soft. 2. Have the ingredients at room temperature not straight out of the fridge. 3. Use self raising flour. 4. Size 2 eggs are best. 5. Don't bake in too hot an oven.

Cake Making Methods.

Rubbing In: Normally used for fruit cakes. The flour and butter is rubbed together into fine breadcrumbs, the fruit, eggs etc are then added.

Whisking: Swiss roll and gateau sponges. Usually fatless. The eggs and sugar are whisked over the saucepan of hot water until trebled in volume. The flour is very carefully folded in.

Creaming: Victoria Sponge, and the most popular method of cake making. Fat and sugar is beaten together until light and fluffy. Then the eggs are gradually beaten in. The flour is carefully folded in at the end.

Melting: Gingerbread. Butter, sugar, syrup and liquid are melted together with the fruit, cooled slightly, then the flour is stirred in to make a batter.

Apple and Almond Cake

For an extra treat serve with clotted cream. This is a rubbing in method.

8oz-225gm self raising flour
4oz-110gm butter
3 eggs, beaten
2 medium bramley cooking apples, peeled and diced
1/2 tspn salt
8oz-225gm castor sugar
1oz-25gm chopped almonds
demerara sugar to sprinkle on top

1...Sieve flour and salt together.
2...Rub in the butter to make fine breadcrumbs.
3...Add the castor sugar, almonds and chopped apple and mix thoroughly.
4...Add the beaten eggs and mix well.
5...Turn the mixture into an 8" buttered cake tin and sprinkle the demerara sugar over the top.
6.. Bake in a pre-heated oven, 200c/400f/gas6 for 1 hour. Cool on a wire rack.

Serves 8.

From the kitchen of...

Mincemeat and Nut Tart

3.1/2oz-100gm butter melted
8oz-225gm digestive biscuits crushed
4oz-110gm walnut pieces roughly chopped
1lb-450gm good quality mince meat
2oz-50gm raisins
1oz-25gm arrowroot
3fl oz-75ml orange juice

10"-26cm loose bottomed flan ring

1...Mix together the melted butter and crushed biscuit and press into the
bottom and sides of the lightly greased flan ring.
2...Set the oven to 190c/350f/gas5.
3...In a saucepan gently simmer together the walnuts, mincemeat, raisins in
3/4pt-400ml water for about 10 minutes. (Not too long)
4...Dissolve the arrowroot in the orange juice and add to the fruit and nut
mixture. Return to the heat and simmer until the mixture thickens. Do not boil
or the mixture will turn thin again. Turn the mixture into the biscuit base and
bake for 10 minutes.
Cool thoroughly. Remove the loose flan ring and serve with whipped cream

N.B. Brandy or whisky can be used instead of orange juice.

Chocolate and Chestnut Roulade

4 large eggs
4oz-110gm castor sugar
3oz-75gm self-raising flour
1oz-25gm cocoa powder
filling
1/2pt-275ml double cream
1 or 2 tbls brandy
1 small tin sweetened chestnut puree

1...Line and grease a swiss roll tin approx 12"x9"-30.5x23cm and pre-heat oven to 190c375f/gas5.

2...Break the eggs into a mixing bowl. Add the sugar and whisk until light and foamy. This will take about 8-10 minutes using an electric whisk.

3...When the egg and sugar mixture is pale and creamy very carefully fold the sifted flour and cocoa. It is essential that you maintain the bulkiness of the mixture.

4...Pour into the swiss roll tin and lightly level the surface. Bbake in the pre-heated oven for 15-20 minutes or until the centre is firm and springy.

5...Lay a piece of greaseproof paper on the work surface and sprinkle with castor sugar. Losen the edges of the sponge and turn out onto the greaseproof paper. With a sharp knife cut off the outside edges off the sponge, then while still hot roll the sponge up.

6...Filling: mix together the chestnut puree and brandy. Whip the double cream and fold into the chestnut mixture. When the sponge is cold, unroll, spread over the chestnut cream and re-roll.

7...Dredge generously with icing sugar. Keep in the fridge until ready to serve.

This is also delicious served as a dessert with chocolate sauce.

Christmas in the New Forest

You might not see Father Christmas drawn along in a sleigh by reindeers but it is quite likely that you will see him pulled through the New Forest villages in a horse and cart. There is a rich community of villages in the Forest and this is just a small example of the village life that whirls around the Forest. It is so indicative of an old fashioned Christmas.

Although snow does fall in the south, its staying power has little to commend it and the picture post card of white coated ponies and frosted lacy branches soon melts away. Not so the seasonal festivities. Dreaming of Christmas in the New Forest conjures up pictures of blazing log fires, Wellington boots, hushed forest walks following in the footsteps of deep animal tracks. Hot punch and a bounty of wonderful festive flavours. Whether you are cooking the yuletide feast yourself or sampling that specially created Christmas menu at your favourite restaurant, and there is no shortage of choice.

If you are planning to spend Christmas in the New Forest, or are this year going to treat your family to Christmas Day lunch out, be sure to book well in advance. Don't forget the New Forest has a national reputation for its good food and people are prepared to travel from afar to sample it. If Christmas is to be spent at home get your orders for that haunch of venison, side of ham, plump turkey or goose, and other local specialities, home made mince pies, Christmas cakes and puddings, placed while stocks last.

Chocolate and Apricot Flapjacks

2 tbls clear honey
6oz-175gm margarine
4oz-110gm light soft brown sugar
8oz-225gm rolled oats
3oz-75gm ready to eat apricots, cut into small pieces
3oz-75gm plain chocolate chips

1...Pre-heat the oven to 180c/350f/4gas. Grease and line a 7" baking tin.
2...Place the honey, margarine and sugar in a saucepan and melt over a low heat.
3...Stir in the oats, apricots and chocolate chips.
4...Pour the mixture into the tin. Level and press down.
5...Cook for 30-35 minutes until just firm.
6...Leave to set (about thirty minutes) and cut into slices.

From the menu of...

THE BROCK AND BRUIN TEAROOM
25 Brookley Road. Brockenhurst. Hants. Tel: 01590 622020
Proprietors: Jane and Graham Overall
Chef: Jane Overall and Sarah Buck
Open: All year. 10am - 6pm. Closed Christmas.
Licensed. Non-smoking. Casual callers and children welcome.
Enjoy delicious home cooking amongst the badgers and bears. A wide range of home-made cakes as well as their own traditionally hand-made fudge and their own chutneys, jams and marmalades.

Blackberry Scones

8oz-225gm self raising flour
1 tspn bi-carb
1/2 tspn salt
large pinch cinnamon
2oz-50gm butter or margarine
2oz-50gm granulated sugar
4oz-110gm blackberries
1/4pt-150ml creamy milk
1 small egg, beaten
milk and demerara sugar for glazing

1...Pre-heat oven 200c/400f/gas7
2...In a large mixing bowl sift together the flour, bi-carb, salt and cinnamon.
3...Rub in the butter until the mixture resembles fine breadcrumbs.
4...Stir in the sugar and then the blackberries. Mix in the egg and enough milk to make a soft but not sticky dough.
5...Gather the mixture together and briefly and lightly knead into a ball. Flatten out this ball and place on an oiled baking sheet. Flatten out. Brush with milk and sprinkle over the demerara sugar. Score the dough into eight segments (not all the way through). Bake for 20-25 minutes or until golden.
6...Cool. Serve with rich country butter and crab apple jelly.

N.B. other fruits can be used such as diced apple, blueberries, banana.

Crab Apple Jelly

Fruit jellies should be bright and clear, therefore, patience is required. They require a high pectin content and most wild fruits do have this. The amount of sugar required depends upon the amount of juice extracted from the cooked fruit.

4lb-crab apples
3 pints water
sugar (1lb-450gm sugar per pint of fruit juice)

1...Wash the fruit and roughly chop. Leave on the peel but remove any brown damaged bits.
2...Put the crab apples and water in a preserving pan and simmer slowly for about 1 hour until the fruit has cooked to a pulp and the liquid has reduced by approximately one third.
3...Set up your jelly bag with clean bowl underneath. Pour in the fruit pulp and leave to strain over night. It is absolutely essential that you don't squeeze the jelly bag otherwise the juice will become cloudy.
4...Measure the juice and the appropriate amount of preserving sugar. Put into a clean preserving pan. Bring gently to the boil stirring all the time until the sugar has dissolved. Now boil rapidly for 10-12 minutes or until setting point is reached. Take the pan off the heat remove the scum and our into sterilised jars while still hot. Seal immediately and leave to set.

To test setting point. a) put a dessert spoon of the jelly on a cold sauce and put in the fridge for 5 minutes. Remove from the fridge and push your finger against the jelly. if thick ripples form it is ready to bottle.
b) Use a sugar thermometer and when 103c is reached the jelly is ready.

Fresh Lemon Cake

6oz-175gm soft margarine
6oz-175gm fine castor sugar
3 x size 3 eggs
6oz-175gm self-raising flour
1 large lemon plus the juice of half a lemon
8oz-225gm icing sugar.
4oz-110gm margarine

2…Whisk together the castor sugar and soft margarine until white and fluffy.
3…Sift the flour and beat the eggs. Whisk in a third of the beaten egg and a teaspoon of the flour. Repeat until all the egg is used up. Add the finely grated rind of the lemon. Mix well. Then carefully fold in the flour.
4…Divide the cake mixture between the two 7" sponge tins, level and make a slight indent in the centre of each. Bake for 25-30 minutes until risen and firm in the centre. Turn out onto a wire rack to cool.
5…While the cake is still warm prick all over and pour over the juice of the lemon.
6…Beat together the margerine and sifted icing sugar and the juice of half a lemon until light and fluffy. Use half of it to sandwich the cake together.
7…Spread the rest of the lemon butter icing over the top of the cake and mark a pattern with the tip of a pointed knife.

From the kitchen of…

SPLASHES TEA SHOP
37 Brookley Road. Brockenhurst. Hants. Tel: 01590 622120
Proprietor: Vivien and Robert
Chef: Vivien
Open: All year. Hours 9am - 5.30pm Monday to Saturday. Sunday 10am - 6pm. All welcome.
Delicious specialities. Vegetarian dishes Home-made cakes and freshly baked scones with fresh cream.

Coffee and Walnut Cake

6oz-175gm fine castor sugar
6oz-175gm soft margarine
3x size three eggs
6oz-175gm self-raising flour
1oz-25gm ground walnuts
1 tbls instant coffee dissolved in 2 tbls hot water
4oz-110gm butter
8oz-225gm icing sugar
1 tbls instant coffee dissolved in 2 tbls hot water, cooled
chopped walnuts for decoration

1...Oil and flour two 7" sponge tins. Pre-heat oven to 180c/350f//gas4.
2...Whisk together the castor sugar and soft margarine until white and fluffy.
3...Beat the eggs and sift the flour. Add a third of the egg mixture to the creamed butter and 1 hpd tspn flour. Repeat until all the egg is used up. Whisk in the cold dissolved coffee.
4...Fold in the sifted flour and ground nuts. Divide the mixture between the two sponge tins. Level off and make a shallow indent in the centre. Bake for 25-30 minutes until the sponge is springy to the touch in the centre. Turn out on to a wire rack and cool.
5...To make the filling. Soften the butter. Add the sifted icing sugar and dissolved coffee and whisk until light and fluffy. Use half of the icing to sandwich the cake together and spread the rest on top. Sprinkle over the chopped walnuts.

Towns and Villages in the Forest

Beaulieu. On the banks of the Beaulieu river and a popular destination for yachtspeople. Set amongst leafy woods and rolling hills.
Montague Arms ** Hazelcopse Bakery and PYO.

Blackfield. On the outskirts of Fawley where the Esso oil refinery is situated. Geologists consider the New Forest to be a likely area for oil excavation.
Taz Indian Brazzerie

Brockenhurst. The perfect place to see the ponies and donkeys ambling along the main street. This village is almost in the centre of the Forest and close to many of the most popular walks.
Splashes Tea Shop ** The Brock and Bruin Tearoom ** Balmer Lawn Hotel Restaurant ** Mange Tout Catering.

Bramshaw. A delightful village with a typical village green in its centre, it is set amongst dense woodlands. The verges garzed by pigs, donkeys and ponies.
The Bell Inn

Bucklers Hard. Set on the banks of the Beaulieu river. The ships for Nelsons fleet were built here in the 18th Century. Cruises along the river can be taken from here also a delightful river side walk.
The Master Builder's House restaurant or public bar.

Burley. If you are a horseriding enthusiast then this is the village for you. A delightful village with several stables and plenty of open heathland ideal for a good gallop.
Toad Hall Hotel-Restaurant ** The Queens Head

Dibden This tiny hamlet rests in the countryside between Southampton water and The Forest's edge.
Gleneagles Pub

Emery Down. A hamlet well know for its trout fisheries. An area surrounded by well known forest walks and the arboretum planted with some rare trees.
The New Forest Inn

Fawley/Ashlett. Well off the beaten-track. Ashlett Creek nestles in a wooded valley on the edge of Southampton Water. An old tidal mill gives this quay side village its old English charm.
The Jolly Sailor

Fordingbridge. Set on the river Avon and steeped in history. It has a mention in the Domesday Book and its Medieval seven-arched bridge sets the scene of this small town which maintains that genuine Olde England atmosphere.
The Lions Court Hotel-Restaurant ** The George Inn.

Hythe/Hythe Marina. On the Eastern edge of The Forest and a little off the beaten-track. Close to Southampton Water a regular ferry service takes you across to Southampton's Royal Pier. Hythe's pier is over one hundered years old..
The Boat House ** The Croft Tavern

Lymington. Port to the Isle of Wight Ferry, and a popular stopping place for sailors. A small town that is always buzzing. There's an open market in the high street every Saturday and plenty of gift shops and places to eat.
Bosuns Chair ** Monet's Bistro ** Hallmark Outside Catering

Lyndhurst. Once a small rural village, now considered the capital of the New Forest. Home of the Queens House and where the Verderers carry out their important work.
Court House Tearooms ** The Swan Inn

Netley Marsh. On the North side of the Forest and links up with
J J's Desserts (caterers)

Redlynch. A small town on the way to Salisbury.
Pensworth Farms(suppliers)

Sway. A small rural village but important enough to have a railway station there. It is positioned on the very edge of the Forest.
Carriages Restaurant at The String of Horses ** The Forest Heath Hotel.

Index of Contributors

Cafes and Tearooms

12/84   Brock and Bruin Tearoom. Brockenhurst. Tel: 01590 622020
  87   Splashes Tea Shop. Brockenhurst. Tel: 01590 622120
  80   The Court House. Lyndhurst. Tel: 01703 283871

Caterers

  75   Hallmark Catering. Lymington. Tel: 01590 675506
  76   J J's Desserts. Netley Marsh Workshops. 01703 660814
  12   Mange - Tout Catering. Brockenhurst. Tel: 01590 622020

Public Houses

  24   Bell Inn, The. Brook. 01703 812214
  27   Bosuns Chair. Lymington. Tel: 01590 675140
  32   Croft Tavern, The. Hythe. Tel: 01703 842141
  62   George Inn, The. Fordingbridge. Tel: 01425 652040
  35   Gleneagles. Hythe. Tel: 01703 842162
21/56   Jolly Sailor. Ashlett Creek. Tel: 01703 891305
20/46   New Forest Inn. Emery Down. Tel: 01703 282329
  14   Queen's Head, The. Burley. Tel: 01425 403423
17/50   String of Horses. Sway. Tel: 01590 682631
  59   Swan Inn. Lyndhurst. Tel: 01703 282203

Note to Businesses
If you cook your own speciality dishes,
or if you run a speciality shop,
or sell or manufacture a local product or ingredient
and would like to be featured in the next edition
of this book, please contact
Travelling Gourmet Publications

Producers and Suppliers

28 Lymore Valley Herbs.
65 Lymington Wine.
72 New Forest Cider.
30 Pensworth Dairy. Redlynch. Tel: 01725 510437
71 Hazelcopse Farm Shop/Bakery/PYO. Beaulieu. Tel: 01590 612696

Restaurants/Bistros/Brasseries

64 Balmer Lawn Hotel/Restaurant. Brockenhurst. Tel: 01590 623116
22/38 Boat House, The. Hythe Marina. Tel: 01703 845594
17/50 Carriages Restaurant. Sway. Tel: 01590 682631
48 Forest Heath Hotel/Restaurant. Sway. Tel: 01590 682287
55 Lion's Court Restaurant. Fordingbridge. Tel: 01425 652006
42 Master Builders House. Bucklers Hard. Tel: 01590 616253
60 Montagu Arms Hotel/Restaurant. Beaulieu. Tel: 01590 612324
40 Monte's Brasserie. Lymington. Tel: 01590 672007
53 Taz Indian Brasserie. Blackfield. Tel: 01703 898218/891013
61 Toad Hall Restaurant. Burley. Tel: 01425 633448

Conversion Tables

All these are *approximate* conversions which have either been rounded up or down. In a few recipes it has been necessary to modify them very slightly. Never mix metric and imperial measurements in one recipe; stick to one system or the other

WEIGHTS

$^1/_2$ oz	10 g
1	25
$1^1/_2$	40
2	50
3	75
4	110
5	150
6	175
7	200
8	225
9	250
10	275
12	350
13	375
14	400
15	425
1 lb	450
$1^1/_4$	550
$1^1/_2$	700
2	900
3	1.4kg
4	1.8
5	2.3

VOLUME

1 fl oz	25 ml
2	50
3	75
5 ($^1/_4$ pint)	150
10 ($^1/_2$)	275
15 ($^3/_4$)	400
1 (pint)	570
$1^1/_4$	700
$1^1/_2$	900
$1^3/_4$	1 litre
2	1.1
$2^1/_4$	1.3
$2^1/_2$	1.4
$2^3/_4$	1.6
3	1.75
$3^1/_4$	1.8
$3^1/_2$	2.0
$3^3/_4$	2.1
4	2.3
5	2.8
6	3.4
7	4.0
8 (1 gal)	4.5

MEASUREMENTS

$^1/_4$ inch	0.5 cm
$^1/_2$	1.0
1	2.5
2	5.0
3	7.5
4	10.0
6	15.0
7	18.0
8	20.5
9	23.0
11	28.0
12	30.5

OVEN TEMPERATURE

Mark 1	275°F	140°C
2	300	150
3	325	170
4	350	180
5	375	190
6	400	200
7	425	220
8	450	230
9	475	240

Index of Recipes

Apple and almond cake 80
Apple and blackberry sorbet 69
Ashlett Smokie 21

Baked egg and smoked ham en cocotte 31
Beef fillet, Carriages 50
Blackberry scones 85
Blanket of pork with capers and paprika 52
Braised beef in Guinness 48

Carib chicken 56
Chicken korma 53
Chilli on fire 35
Chocolate and apricot flapjacks 84
Chocolate and chestnut roulade 82
Cider and apple upside down tart 72
Coffee and walnut cake 88
Colcannon 49
Crab apple jelly 86
Croft lasagne 32

Dairy quiche 30
Duck pot 58
Duck, Marinated 60

Fillet of Beef Carriages 50
Filo scallop shell 40
Fresh lemon cake 87
Fresh water eels in tomato sauce 44
Forester's burger 36

Goosberry and elderflower crush 73

Ham in white wine and grape sauce 66
Hazelnut meringue roulade with toffee cream 76

Lasagne, Croft, 32
Leeks and ham au gratin 34
Lemon cake, fresh 87
Lemon rock cakes 78
Lions Court supreme of chicken 54
Lymington wine ham 66

Mincemeat and nut tart 81
Marinated duck 60
Mushroom barquette 17
Mushroom and marjoram soup 19
Mussels, Wessex 20

New Forest pasty 24

Parsnip and peanut soup 12
Pesto sauce 28
Pheasant in apple and celery sauce 62
Pizza tart 1990 29
Pork with capers and paprika 52
Prawn Creole 27
P.Y.O pudding 71

Quail stuffed with spinach and mushrooms 61
Quiche, dairy 30

Ragout of venison with caramelised apple 64
Roast supreme of chicken 54

Salmon, baked, with ginger sauce 41
Salmon, fillet, on a bed of spring vegetables 38
Salmon gratinee 42
Saute d'agnueau frambroise 46
Scallops in basil butter sauce 22
Scallop, filo shells 40
Spiced parsnip and peanut soup 12
Swan's special duck pot 58

Tuscan pie 26

Upside down apple and cider tart 72

Venison ragout with caramelised apples 64
Watercress soup 14
Watercress tartlets with stilton sauce 16
Wessex mussels 20
White chocolate truffle cake and coffee cream 74
Wild mushroom and marjoram soup 19

Notes